E(3)

"The Barnabas Touch"

Three Secrets to Successful Leadership

* Encourage * Empower * Engage *

SUSAN FARAH

BALBOA.
PRESS

A DIVISION OF HAY HOUSE

Balboa Press books may be ordered through booksellers or by contacting:

Balboa Press
A Division of Hay House
1663 Liberty Drive
Bloomington, IN 47403
www.balboapress.com
1 (877) 407-4847

Because of the dynamic nature of the Internet, any web addresses or links contained in this book may have changed since publication and may no longer be valid. The views expressed in this work are solely those of the author and do not necessarily reflect the views of the publisher, and the publisher hereby disclaims any responsibility for them.

The author of this book does not dispense medical advice or prescribe the use of any technique as a form of treatment for physical, emotional, or medical problems without the advice of a physician, either directly or indirectly. The intent of the author is only to offer information of a general nature to help you in your quest for emotional and spiritual well-being. In the event you use any of the information in this book for yourself, which is your constitutional right, the author and the publisher assume no responsibility for your actions.

Any people depicted in stock imagery provided by Thinkstock are models, and such images are being used for illustrative purposes only.
Certain stock imagery © Thinkstock.

Printed in the United States of America.

ISBN: 978-1-5043-2511-0 (sc)
ISBN: 978-1-5043-2512-7 (e)

Balboa Press rev. date: 01/21/2015

This book is dedicated to everyone and everything that stood in my way – <u>thank you</u>!

Without you, I never would have made it!

Susan

Contents

Prologue ix

The Barnabas Touch xiii

Secret #1 – Engage xv

Secret #2 – Encouragement xxi

Secret #3 – Empower xxvii

Chapter 1 – Working with Individuals 1

Chapter 2 – Working with a Team 14

Chapter 3 – Working with Your Contemporaries 25

Chapter 4 – Working with Your Leader (Boss) 40

Chapter 5 – Working with the Enemy – You 43

Chapter 6 – Boundaries in Leadership 47

Chapter 7 – Problems Common to Leadership 49

Chapter 8 – "Call-ins for Dummies…" 55

Chapter 9 – Are you an Olympian? 57

Chapter 10 – Troubleshooting – Interviews 60

The End of the Beginning… 67

What Next? 71

Epilogue 73

Appendix 77

Prologue

I believe there are both a "leader" *and* a "follower" inside each one of us.

At any given time we can be either. We can even switch back and forth as the situation dictates, but ultimately we will be one of them. Because if you are not leading you are following and if you are not following someone else, you are leading – even if the only one you are leading is "you" and the direction of your life.

The important question to you now is: "Did *you* make the choice?" "Or did you not?"

How about these questions: *"Are there natural born leaders?"* Or, do great leaders need to be molded and shaped and then spend a lifetime working extremely hard to maintain it?

"Is it experience that makes a great leader?"

"Does age matter?"

"What are the qualities of a great leader?"

And the list goes on and on...

But, I want to know - who decides? Who separates the good leaders from the bad and the good ones from the great ones?

And, who put *them* in charge of this deciding anyway?

I have learned just as much over the years from bad leaders (bosses), than I have from the good ones, maybe more. I knew I didn't want to be like them that's for sure (the bad ones), and I definitely didn't enjoy working for them at the time. Many of you may have experienced this same thing.

Volumes of books have been written on styles of leadership and how to become a good leader. Books written on how to influence people and how to work with difficult people, *this book isn't one of those.*

This book isn't to turn you into something you aren't.

This book is about who you *already are.* This book is about one thing. That one thing is E(3) – *the three secrets to successful leadership,* the same three secrets that lead to *successful relationships* and the same three secrets that lead to a *successful life.*

They may be simple in content but can be difficult to execute. That's the catch.

Ironic, isn't it?

And even though these three secrets will be used by many people the outcomes can be very different because each leader is a unique individual. So, if you are hoping to be exactly like Donald Trump or Steve Jobs or some great executive of some great company, you will be greatly disappointed.

You can't. You can't duplicate someone else.

*But the good news is **that is** the good news.*

In fact, it's great news because you have the potential to be even more successful. Your successful leadership - the one that only you can be - the one that only you can create and execute is waiting for you!

How do I know this? I know because we are all born with limitless potential and because, I have lived it.

This probably is a good place to tell you a little bit about myself. People usually want to know something about the author of the book that they are about to read. What makes that person qualified enough to spend money on their book and spend their precious time reading and listening for the meaning in those words.

Well let's see, I have managed, mentored and coached for over twenty five years, started and ran a successful non-profit 501c3 for ten years, created incredibly productive teams and have had enough bosses (the good, the bad and the ugly), to last me a lifetime.

I have managed as few as one and as many as 200. And since I believe we take everything we have learned and then put it to good use in our next adventure - I, at this point, have a lot of really great stuff to share with you.

Have I passed the test?

Are you ready?

And has this made you as excited as I am to begin?

If so, *"Come on, follow my lead"*

The Barnabas Touch

"Encouragement is the glue that holds everything together..."

- Susan Farah

It's true. Look at any situation. Look at any relationship – personal or business. It started with encouragement – a smile, a nod, a handshake – maybe even a "hello". Now keep looking. Any friendship, employment or partnership that has lasted is only still working because of *encouragement.*

Barnabas signifies and exemplifies encouragement. In fact, Barnabas literally means *"Son of Encouragement."* Look it up, you will find the story of Barnabas in the bible throughout the Book of Acts. And it is through this example that the framework for our goal; *successful leadership,* will be formed.

Barnabas was one of the first to sell his possessions to help the ministry, *making an investment in others.* First to travel with the Apostle Paul as a missionary, *he was* willing to *engage others, be fully involved and put his needs last.* Barnabas *risked his life and his reputation for what he believed in.* As a result he quietly became one of the most influential people of his time. Without Barnabas we can only wonder what might have happened to the forward progress of the ministry.

I am sure encouragement itself was around a long time before, but it is at this point where it becomes clear that one's life can be measured through the accomplishments of others, not just through the accomplishments of one's self. It is only through the improvements and successes of others that true encouragement can be discovered and measured. This is why I chose "The Barnabas Touch" for the title of this book. It is my strong belief in the validity and integrity of encouragement and the knowledge that without it - it is impossible to reach others. *This belief* guides me and pushes me onward.

So do you think being a Barnabas, having the *"Barnabas Touch"*, is important enough for you?

When we read about the lives of great men and women we find they all have something in common; *encouragers* - they had them in all shapes, sizes and disguises along the way. If those encouragers hadn't been there doing their job, outcomes would have been radically different. Without their encouragers, *"Would these great men and women truly have been that great?"*

Without encouragement from someone who believed in them, *"Would they have become that "person of influence?" "Would they have had the confidence in themselves to accomplish what they did?"*

Let's go one step further, let's say that encouragement is influence and influence, is power.

Encouragement   **Influence**   **Power**

Advocacy = Trust = Loyalty

So, if encouragement is the influence and power that holds everything together, then it sounds to me like encouragement is the keystone - the very bedrock of successful leadership, the glue.

And this encouragement is the foundation on which we will build our success.

It is important for you to keep this in the forefront of your mind as you read further and we discover together, the *"Three Secrets of Successful Leadership"*.

Secret #1 - Engage

Have I confused you or just surprised you?

Did you think that Secret #1 was going to be encouragement? Well, even though encouragement is our foundation and the base that we will build on, it is not the first critical concept we must master. Before we encourage we must engage and not just engage; but we must fully understand what engage means, what it entails and be able to master the art of it – the *"art of engagement"*.

If you are reading this book then you are seeking ways to be a better leader. You are searching for a formula or a step-by-step "how-to" for successful leadership. Then it is important for us to first define leadership.

Wikipedia defines leadership as a *"process of social influence in which one person can enlist the aid and support of others in the accomplishment of a common task"*.

You will notice several key phrases in that definition; <u>enlist</u> the aid and support of others and the accomplishment of a <u>common</u> task - neither of which can be done without engaging.

This tells us that leadership must rely on the engagement of individuals. So it stands to reason that the better the engagement the better (and more successful), the leadership.

The Encarta dictionary – English (NA) tells us that to engage means to; *require the use of or the devotion of something, to <u>involve</u> somebody or become involved, attract somebody or <u>hold the attention</u> of somebody, to fight somebody and thus begin a battle and lastly, to <u>interlock</u> and bring something <u>together</u>.* I am including all of these definitions because they are all meaningful to our purpose.

Immediately my mind goes to "interlock and bring something together". To engage we must interlock and *connect* with someone else. Not just make some idle small talk and ten seconds later can't remember the conversation or even the person.

Engaging entails giving of yourself – *you must give something of yourself away.* It is not just taking from someone else for your own private purpose - that would be *sales.* This is leadership – *successful leadership.*

Before you can become a better leader or at least a more successful one you must be in touch with yourself. For our purpose you must engage yourself first. Do you really want to be a leader? Is this something that you are choosing to do or has it been thrust upon you? The answer to that question will determine whether you are in conflict with yourself: excitement and joy *versus* duty and responsibility.

Are you doing it for the money, power or prestige? Again, the answer will determine your motive.

If you don't understand your motive, you don't understand yourself and you won't be able to understand the followers you are hoping to accumulate like so many grains of sand on the beach. I am not saying you can't be a successful leader if it is the money or power or even the duty that motivates you - *but unless you know who you are - no one is going to follow you, or at least not for long.*

You will have people confused as to who they are following – one day they will be following Ghandi and the next day they will be following Attila the Hun. Quite a difference there don't you think? The rollercoaster ride will be too rough, they will fall off, fall away and *go* away - leaving you standing there holding your sword, *all alone.*

So be honest with yourself.

If it is power and money you want then you will have to keep your urge in check to see people as only the end to your means – as just objects, (robots) doing your bidding so you can reach your goals. People are not objects or robots - they have to eat and breathe and sleep and pay their bills, too.

If you are a leader and trying to be one out of a sense of duty or because it has fallen in your lap and you don't know how to get out of it. Then you will need to curb your urges to resent who you are leading, why you are leading them and yourself - for compromising and not standing up for yourself, (if that is what you think you have done).

And just because you want to be a leader to make a difference, give back and help others, does not get you off the hook. You will need to keep yourself on a very strong leash not to be an enabler and "the nice guy" or "one of the gang", or else you will really mess things up! You will steal the opportunity for your followers to learn from their mistakes and grow the strength *they need to succeed.*

It's kind of like the story of "Goldilocks and the Three Bears". Remember the porridge? First it was too hot and then it was too cold and then it was just right. *We are after that porridge balance – the "just right".*

So let's say you have taken a look inside, figured yourself out and realize why you are or why you want to be a leader. And now you are ready to do everything you can to be a good and a successful one.

The next thing you need to ask yourself is "Why am I putting myself through this, and do I understand" – that no matter what I do half of the people won't like it or like me. Many will think they know more than I do, many will resent me for no reason and the other half will resent me because I have given them a reason to. They will smile to my face and talk about me behind my back, they will gossip about me, they will lie about me, they will try to sabotage me, they will ignore me and resist me, they will try to "smooze me" (brown-nose), and they will try to get my job because they actually think it is easier to lead rather than to follow.

Are you sure you still want to be a leader?

If you have answered "Yes", read on...

You have engaged yourself or at least you know your goal is to be a successful leader and you understand your motive behind your choice. Now, I mentioned before the trick to this first secret is in the "art of engagement" - so now it's time to learn the basic principle behind it, *love*.

You can lead all day but if you want people to follow you have to love people.

Remember I didn't say you had to *like them* – I said you had to *love them*, big difference.

You can't lead anything if you hate it. You can push it around or you can bend it until it breaks but that is not leadership. That's intimidation, fear and terrorism – *any fool can do that!*

You have to accept or at least come to the conclusion that people are not perfect, they are just in different stages of development and improvement and *you* are meeting them somewhere along their path. You can either help them get to the next level or if you can't help them you need to not get in their way, let them pass – someone else will help them.

They may disappoint you, so your job is to have enough self esteem and self confidence in yourself that your image of *"you"* does not hinge on *"them"*. And at the end of the day you can take the good with the bad and laugh, or better still be able to get a good night's sleep so you can start all over again the next day. And you also understand that you are not perfect either and that these people, your followers – *have to dig real deep to love you, too!*

It is love and acceptance for the human race. No more – no less.

Now wasn't there something I said about not having to "like" them?

True, you don't have to like their personal beliefs, their personal choices, their spouses or anything that is outside of the workplace. It's their life and it results from their choices – you are not responsible for them. Their choices may interfere with their work performance and you may have to deal with that - but you don't' have to like them. *You have to lead them.*

You just have to love what you like, and what you don't like - the "love" is not optional.

What is so important above love?

Love is nonjudgmental. It is not prejudice – two absolutes for successful leadership.

A good leader needs to see people through a "pure eye" – a genuine eye. One that is not clouded with pre-determined ideas, prejudices or intolerances. There has to be a healthy respect for that the person in front of you, because they are no more or less a human being than you are. The two of you may be very different, *but they have the same right as you do to exist.*

The "art of engagement" is being able to automatically - talk, interview, discuss, teach, correct, delegate and evaluate all kinds of individuals fairly and equally; ultimately doing what is best for "them" and for "the company" without thinking about yourself or any selfish motives you might have.

Can you do it?

It truly is an art because it doesn't come naturally to us humans. We have to fight daily the prejudices, fears and negativisms – but it is possible and it is necessary for leadership, and for life.

Ready to review?

We talked about the definitions of engage; 1) to interlock and bring something together – *that is you and your followers,* 2) require the use of or devotion – *that is your followers with the confidence in you to let you lead them,* 3) attract or hold the attention of – *this is your leadership in action* and, 4) to fight somebody and begin the battle – *this is reality,* (my personal favorite).

That somebody is *you,* and you will be in a battle every day you have chosen leadership as your vocation.

Leadership – your "badge of **c-c-courage**".

Secret #2 - Encouragement

The first thing you must remember is that you have been where they are. Or have you forgotten?

Your first job – you weren't the boss, right?

You had a boss. Many of you even had several of them. So close your eyes and remember what it felt like to walk into a situation and not know anyone or what was expected of you.

What did it really feel like? Were you scared, intimidated and wanting to throw up? Or maybe you just wanted to run out the door. Maybe you were the one that stuck out your chest and pretended you knew more than everyone else to hide your true feelings. Because as a leader these very feelings with bodies attached to them will show up at your doorstep and *you* will be expected not only to *lead them - but to be successful at it.*

How can you do that unless you can understand them? To remember what it was like to *be them*. The solution is, "don't forget", visualize yourself in their shoes.

What would you be hearing and seeing if you were them - staring up at you?

What would *you* be thinking of *you*?

What are your words saying and what is the tone behind those words? Does it match up or is it conveying two different things? Is what you are saying to them clear or are you already two steps ahead in your head and there's *no way* they can catch up?

Been there – done that. A little story...

As a child I wanted to be a teacher or at least that is what I thought. In high school I joined "Future Teachers" and remember having my picture taken for the yearbook. But that is all I remember about it. Obviously much didn't rub off because it took me years to realize I wasn't a teacher and because of that I was interfering with others' ability to succeed in their tasks. I hadn't given them all the tools they needed – *I wasn't explaining it right.* I knew it in my head but it got lost somewhere between there and it's destination – *them.*

In my first real supervisory position I put out a memo to the entire facility, approximately 200 people and totally insulted them. I didn't know I insulted them until my boss, the administrator, came to me and asked, "Did you know that just about everyone in this facility is mad at you?"

Of course, I didn't. I was already on to the next thing.

He showed me my memo and told me to read it as if I were one of the staff I had written it for. It took me well into the second reading before it hit me. What I had written and what I had meant to write - *were two totally different things.*

Revelation! I *had* insulted them.

That was my wake-up call and began an excruciating time of slowing down, asking for advice and testing out my ideas *before* I wrote them for all to see, or stood up in front of the group and shouted them out. But it paid off. I learned to think, *really* think before I acted. And it was the beginning of the journey of becoming a successful leader.

So how does this relate to encouragement?

Because, it's all about them, it's not all about you.

And if you can't teach, motivate, inspire and get the cooperation of who ever it is you are trying to lead - you, them and it (the project), won't succeed. It will fail or best be mediocre. You will fail.

So what is encouragement and why do I believe it is so critical that it has been pegged as our foundation?

Well, a successful leader is just not successful for a minute. And I'm sure you don't want to just be successful for a minute either. You are looking for what all great leaders have - a career full of successes. So, to get others to *continue* to follow you again and again, you must give them a reason to - o*therwise they will stop following you and start following someone else.* That someone else could be the worst employee you've got or even the leader down the street, your competitor who is giving them what they need.

Contrary to popular belief that "something they need" is not more money. That thing they need is *inspiration, motivation, recognition and honest relevant information* – i.e. encouragement.

Encouragement is what *you* wanted and needed when you were a plebe on *your* first job. That trainee, you remember, trying so hard not to mess up and literally drooling for a kind word or a compliment - that *"good job"* from the boss.

Did you get it? If so, how did it make you feel?

If not, how did you feel about them, the company and yourself?

This is why encouragement and "encouragement in action" which is the development of people - is what *all successes hinge on.* You can't have success without people or at least one person and some fancy inventions. Which were, (hello) created by successful people who I am sure "were encouraged by someone" - or else they would have given up.

See?

Remember last chapter when we talked about engaging being all about love?

Well, here is your next shocker.

Encouragement is all about - *belief, faith and hope.*

You must have the hope that your followers will learn, improve and succeed. You must have faith that these followers will want to follow you in whatever you are leading them to do. And lastly, you must believe in yourself and that *you are the one* to lead them.

And since you are the one to lead them - *you are the one to encourage them.*

If you think you are a tough business person or a very strong leader and having hope, faith and belief in people seems a bit soft to you - get over it!

If you think being open and pliable enough to succeed as an encourager and lead others to succeed for your successful longevity is soft, *you are confused*. Because it just might be the hardest thing you've done and it will take all the *strength* you can muster to do it.

Again, if you are reading this book then you are looking to be more successful because you feel something is lacking. You have already admitted you are ready to change and ready for a change. So, don't get scared now!

Just as we discussed earlier, engage and its' counterpart, love is not optional. Faith, hope and belief which is encouragements' counterpart – is not optional either. All are prerequisites for successful leadership.

So, just as acceptance is necessary in any program, you must accept that these qualities are ones which have to be developed further for you to be that successful leader you desire to be.

But what if you think you aren't an encourager? Or worse yet, you think you don't have time or, it's all a waste of time?

Well, you better get this erroneous thinking out of your head and get a grip!

Then you need to continue to read as we tackle the third secret and work together to put all of it into practice in such a way that it will guide you through *any* situation you might encounter.

The "how" always follows the "what"...

p.s. - The true secret to encouragement? Encouragement is, *"the spirit of honor".*

This is a double principle; it is a universal principle *and* a biblical one.

The universal principle: we reap what we sow – *can't plant corn and get cotton.*

The biblical principle: we reap what we sow – *plant an encouraging word and God releases a blessing for you, (your encouragement).*

Now *your* encouragement may be a loyal employee, a better job done by that employee or a comment that employee makes to your boss and presto change-o, "collateral" in your management bank account to be used in the future - for a raise, a promotion or a perk. See?

Win-Win-Win!

But, if you plant constant criticism, suspicion and negativity that is exactly what you will get coming back to you in the form of - lying, high absenteeism, laziness and poor work performance.

See?

I was blind and now I see.

Secret #3 - Empower

Now we come to the last layer of our three-layer, triple-decker secret sandwich –

Empower

Have you been thinking ahead and guessed the counterpart for empower already?

No, not yet? Well, let's go ahead and get the suspense out of the way for you right now. And the counterpart is…

Trust

Yup, your goal all along for successful leadership and for being that successful leader has been to engage and encourage your followers to the point where they have become empowered to succeed in the task you have led them in. You have delegated, but you have not delegated in the traditional way – you have empowered.

And in "authoritative delegation", you have reassigned the trust from yourself to them to accomplish the task. You have made an exchange. And in that "transfer of trust" you have allowed yourself to allow *them* do the succeeding, ultimately making *you* a successful leader.

What do you think so far? Is it making sense?

Can you do it? At least are you willing to try?

I hope so.

Our next step will be to look at various situations in which all leaders find themselves and talk about specific examples of good *versus* poor and successful *versus* unsuccessful leaders and leadership.

You see, it's not enough to know the three secrets – the importance is in *how you use them* in each situation that will determine your success as a leader, and the measure of you as a "person of great leadership".

So, put on your helmet, pick up your sword and let's go win us some battles!

<u>The Barnabas Touch</u> – *"Building trust through encouragement"*

Chapter 1

Working with Individuals

Whether you are a first-time leader or a seasoned one, you will only be successful if you *"lead for success"* and to do that you must have the ability to connect to the *"whom"* you are expected to lead. And if you *are* to connect with them you not only need to know *about* them, but you must <u>know</u> them.

Let me give you an example from my own leadership experiences, my bag of "resume builders".

About ten years ago I was hired to head-up a small case management office with seven employees and a caseload of 200 clients. We were one of twelve offices spread throughout the state. At the time I joined we were 12th in documentation compliance, 12th in census growth, 12th in fiscal management and the #1 problem-child they had - due to revolving-door management and various other issues. In less than two years we moved that office from 12th to 2nd **and** #1 in respect from our superiors.

How you ask?

All of them, the string of temporary administrators and "fixers", had focused on the problems not the potentials, a no-win, lose-lose situation.

But by initiating one change; *"focusing on the potentials not the problems"* it then became a win-win situation. We became a *"winning"* operating machine. This is how we did it.

I asked the employees.

It was as simple as that.

I had never worked in the case management field before, I didn't know these people from Adam and I was walking into a hostile, frustrated and sometimes volatile environment. But - the one thing I did know - *is that, "I didn't know anything"*.

And that was exactly how I needed to come across to the staff. Not as the know-it-all who was going to "fix" them but as a concerned person in a management position who had the power to make a change, make a difference and *"give them a voice"*.

The voice is what they wanted – it's what they needed – in fact, *it's all they needed!*

Before that first day when I would be walking through the doors, I prepared myself. I imagined myself as one of those employees – not knowing who would be walking through that door, friend or foe. Not knowing if that person would fire them all or maybe just a few. But either way, *"We'll have our guard up… we'll be on the defensive"*.

And they were. And I knew they would be.

Be prepared!

Next, I prepared a short list of six questions:

> *Tell me little bit about your self.*
>
> *How long have you worked here?*
>
> *Tell me one good thing about this office.*
>
> *Tell me one bad thing/one thing that needs to change in this office.*
>
> *If I had the power to change one thing what would you want it to be?*
>
> *What do you want for your future and how can I help you get there?*

And lastly, I really thought about what I was going to wear, the presence and demeanor I wanted to project, what items I would bring with me and which part of my *"leader personality"* would lead *"me"*.

That first day had to be all about "nothing".

Sound strange? Why?

You can't walk in and think you are in charge.

They have been in charge, baby! So they are going to fight for their territory.

If you walk in wanting to be in charge – you will be trying to take away something they have been holding on to very tightly and you know what will happen? You won't just lose that battle, but you will lose the entire war and you should just quit while you're ahead and look for another job.

So it had to be about nothing – <u>changing</u> nothing.

I spent the day being friendly, meeting people, asking simple questions, watching and observing the flow, the flow of things and who really had the power in that office. I had been told horror stories about one particular case manager who "was the problem and needed to be fired".

Guess what?

She wasn't the problem.

I mean, she was giving them problems – but *"she wasn't the problem"*. I'll get to that later.

I also set up a time with each of them to meet one-on-one, the next day. This was very important. It will be important when you meet with your "problem children". You must have complete privacy when you talk with each one. If you have to meet outside the office, do it.

And remember to let each one know that what they say to you will be confidential, *and mean it!*

<u>*Never, and I do mean never – lie to them.*</u> Make it your "closed-door policy".

We all know what an open-door policy is – well, you need a closed-door policy, too. What they say behind your closed door won't be held against them. Let them know they can vent - *you want them* to *do it there* and not out in the open in front of other staff, clients or customers.

The next day I wore something a bit more casual and put on my "kind but concerned" face. One by one I talked to my staff. And guess what? They all knew what the problem was, they all wanted basically the same thing and every one of them gave me the same answer when it came to the question: "If I, (their leader) could change one thing what would *they* want that *one* thing to be?"

What do you think that one thing was?

They wanted to have what they needed to do their jobs well (and they did want to do their jobs well), and then be appreciated for doing that job and not just yelled at for what they did wrong.

In addition, they all identified the same roadblock that was physically making their job impossible to do. In a nutshell the roadblock was not having the correct information, consistent training, copies of policies and procedures so they could look it up for themselves, a pat (many pats) on the back and someone to do interference for them so the negative put-downs and comments from above would stop. What they needed was for me to eliminate the roadblock.

Condense that down even more to – they wanted to be heard and listened to, they wanted - **respect**.

I could do that.

I did do that. And you know what happened?

It worked! I got their attention. *And I got their respect.*

Oh, and the roadblock? Well, I personally did that part of their job for them.

I figured out a way I could do it, and in the big scheme of things, it totally changed the way they looked at their jobs - plus it got done. And as for me, I just made it a part of my marketing – which *was my job.*

Go figure! A no-brainer! A win-win situation for all of us, and suddenly *we had a team!*

So now it was time for me go to work. To work with each of them on their weak areas, *eliminate the real personnel problem,* plus maintain the cohesiveness of the team.

In other words; *I had to keep their attention!*

Now this is where the mentoring and coaching comes in. You must do both if you are going to be successful, long term. Through the initial interview and subsequent interactions with my staff, I found out what was important to them personally and professionally, what motivated them and what they needed to change (work areas), for them to be successful. Every one of the staff had something that needed "tweaked" and several had "mucho tweaking" to do.

I won't go through every staff member – I will concentrate on the one that my boss wanted me to fire because she said "they" were the problem.

Let's examine Diamond - that's what we will call her since she was definitely a *"diamond in the rough."*

First, the rough parts of Diamond: she spoke without thinking or thinking of the consequences, could be loud and argumentative, unprofessional-looking at times, her documentation was not done on time, numerous complaints from clients and superiors and, "falsely accused" of being the ring-leader - the instigator of the office's problems.

Now the **potential**: she was passionate, street-smart, intelligent with great insight into her clients, wanted to do a good job, a team player in-hiding and extremely loyal.

Since I wanted to keep her and had went precariously out on a climb to convince my boss I didn't need to fire her but *work with her* and that I "knew" she could change – *something* had to change and quickly!

So, I took a step back, looked at the entire situation and decided we had to stop the complaints and then "tone-down" and "professional-up" her appearance - to show enough improvement so we could buy the time we were going to need to fix everything else.

This is where the phrase "bite the bullet" matched up perfectly with my situation. In the "olden days" before anesthesia, doctors who needed to perform surgery would have the patient bite hard on something, (hence, the bullet) while they were sawing off a leg or chopping a hatchet through their arm.

This describes perfectly what I was about to do!

I took Diamond to a private area and asked her friendly but *firmly* if she wanted to continue to work for our office. She assured me she did. I then asked her if she thought she could do the job if she had what she needed to do it. Again, she assured me she could. I let her know that I believed it also.

Now this is the part that has to be 100% their responsibility. They need to make an agreement with you and verbalize that they understand the rewards and consequences of failing and succeeding. There can be no confusion, misunderstanding or "amnesia" claimed. That is why I always have them repeat back to me what they heard and what they understand this agreement to be. And if need be, put it in writing and have them sign it.

So I began to share a sandwich with Diamond.

What?

Did you say a sandwich? You were eating a *sandwich*?

No, I was not eating a sandwich. The better question for you to have asked me was, *"What kind of sandwich was it?"*

It was a "Successful Leader" sandwich and here are the ingredients:

> *You start off with a positive observation you have made regarding the person you are sharing the sandwich with, (this is the bottom slice of bread). Then you tell them the harsh reality, what you need and what you expect them to do, (this is the meat or the P & J). Lastly, you top it off with another positive observation and add one or two encouraging statements, (the top slice of bread).*

You have just created a palatable "bite the bullet" scenario and you didn't have to amputate any body parts or cause the person to "bleed out".

In this case, I told Diamond I admired her passion and it was quite obvious she really cared about her clients and their welfare. This began to put her at ease and acknowledged that I had been observing her and recognized this aspect of her personality.

Now, the inside of the sandwich, the tough part...

I told her there were some things she would need to change so employment with us could continue smoothly. We went on to talk about the tone of her voice and some specific words and phrases that needed to go and ones she could substitute them for. Next was her appearance, this is always a very touchy area – very personal and must be handled with care.

So far things were going fairly well. Her defenses had gone up a little with the inclusion of her appearance, but I remained calm and used real life examples and situations to point out how all this was going to *benefit her.* Time frames of when I expected to see changes happening were given and also a date when we would meet again and compare notes, always keeping her in the loop.

The focus was always on *her* and not the "company". It didn't need to turn into a *"them against me"* drama.

All along I allowed her to vent her feelings but continued to remain in control.

It's important not to let the other person *take the control from you*, get loud or demanding, (that's their defense mechanism if they feel they are being attacked). I realized this was enough "meat" to load on at this time, so I finished the sandwich with reassurance that I would be available to her as she made these changes and repeated several times that, *"I believed she could do it".*

Lastly, I had her repeat back to me what she believed I had asked her to do. This way our expectations would be the same. I can't tell you how many times early on in my managing I had made the mistake of thinking the other person was thinking exactly what I was, when in truth, we were on two totally different planets - light years apart!

Now was the real test. Would she respond by changing or would she go home, begin fuming about it, call the rest of the team and sabotage me.

What do you think happened?

Well, the next day came and in walked Diamond, on time with a totally different look.

And not only a different look but a different attitude, softer voice and a less dramatic demeanor. And of course, I noticed and encouraged her. The more I noticed and encouraged her - the more she tried to make the changes I had asked of her.

Then other people noticed, too. Her peers, outsiders and even my boss made a positive comment – which was a miracle in it's self, as she was the one who wanted to fire Diamond to begin with.

Now don't get me wrong, it wasn't all peaches and cream and we had a few setbacks – but the end result was spectacular.

Another thing I did. Not only did I encourage her at work but I let her know I was interested in her as a person and in her aspirations - and she had some amazing aspirations. She had a dream of working in TV or film – in front of and behind the camera. She was actually in school for this very thing and in her spare time would do stand-up comedy, (she could be a scream).

She also acted in local drama theaters and my husband and I made it a point to go see her on opening nights, take her roses and give them to her after the show. She needed *validation*. Besides, she was *awesome!*

Can you see all the uses of - engage, encourage and empower in the above example?

What would have happened if I had come in and fired Diamond (or any of the others), without first taking the time to make up my own mind about them?

Would I have gotten their respect or would they just have seen me as an extension of "the company".

Would I have been able to gain their trust?

Would I have been the leader they would follow?

Take the time to think through and answer all of these questions before we move on.

<u>REMEMBER</u> – <u>REWARD THE GOOD TO MINIMIZE THE BAD!</u>

My definition of minimize – *don't discipline it unless you really have to and then give the least discipline you can while recognizing, encouraging and publicizing the good until that good <u>is great</u>!*

You know what else I did?

I found out all the correct information, policies, procedures and expectations they needed to have to do their job and made it available to them in several ways. First, a Policy & Procedure book, (no one really looks at this big thing but you must have it there for the bosses and for any credentialing agency).

Secondly, in-services and roundtable discussions, (make time for the venting – if you don't they will vent behind your back and your success will be cut in half). Thirdly, we laminated strategic and critical policies and posted them in places easy for the staff to see and read.

What else did we do? Well, at our weekly meetings we played games, (like Jeopardy) around any new policies and the staff who got the most correct received a prize.

And I care planned with them.

This may not be a process that everyone knows about – care planning is used in healthcare settings. But the point is – we looked at a situation or problem, identified the roadblocks, came up with a solution and an outcome for each roadblock, put a time table to each one, and a date to check and evaluate what we had done to see if we were being successful with our new implementations.

When I say we care planned I don't mean we just talked about it. We used a big poster board and wrote on it in bright colors and added some visual designs/pictures to give it life. And we displayed it in a prominent place in the office for all to see. It was in front of them everyday – in their line of vision and on their mind everyday.

The other thing is - *they* had to come up with the roadblocks and the solutions and the timeframes. *They* had to own it. It was *their* office, *their* problem, *their* solution and *their* success to make, (or not). *Theirs – not mine*!

They had to buy in to it – they had to!

And most importantly I fed them. It really is the most important thing.

Hungry people are mean, cranky, tired, lifeless, thoughtless and suffer from "no" attention span at all!

So I fed them at every meeting and event. I fed them for every occasion, (and we thought of many and any occasions). And I fed them when there was no occasion – just because it was Thursday or Monday or Friday or Wednesday or a Tuesday.

We celebrated birthdays, gave yearly recognition pins, certificates for outstanding client service, and participated in the corporate "recognize an employee each day" email that went out to everyone in the entire corporation.

And when one of them "made it" we posted it and celebrated it!

Oh by the way, it had to be a supervisor who sent these recognitions in. So supervisor, (leader) remember to do it! In the case of our office – supervisors never did before, so there way no way the staff could feel the appreciation, feel the "love".

Something very important to always remember, when you reward or surprise a staff - individualize it.

Make what you *do* give them – *relevant to them.* Make is something *they* want, not generic, like you took no thought in doing it.

I know this may sound like a lot of time and trouble – and it does take time. But if you don't do it, you *will* have trouble and you will have plenty of time because you will be out of a job – and *you* will have done it to yourself. No one to blame but you… the buck stops here.

Now this is what else I did – I took each one of my staff and worked with *them individually* on their rough areas and their potentials until I was able to sustain their respect and trust. It was at this point I believed Diamond and the others were ready for the challenge.

What was the challenge you ask?

The challenge was to get them to do the unrealistic things the "mother ship", (the company) wanted them do.

For us "trekkie" fans think back about every Star Trek movie or episode from the TV series. The Federation, (mother ship) was always faced with an impossible dilemma to try to solve. So, they would contact Captain James T. Kirk of the Starship Enterprise and ask him to go (and take his tired crew), "where no man or woman has gone before". Doc would get upset, Mr. Spock would have his reservations and one or two of the dispensable crew would get eliminated. Then Captain Kirk would come up with a spectacular idea, rally the troops with an awe-inspiring speech and of course, bend the rules a little.

This would allow the group to search and destroy and be victorious - the world would be saved.

Yeah!

Saved to live another day and then have to do it all again the next week or the next millennium – which ever came first.

Sound familiar? Sound like a page from your life?

Well, successful leadership is just like being successful in your life. There will always be a problem. A solution will always have to be found. Someone or several "someone's" will have to do whatever it takes to fix the problem. And everyone lives to fight another day. Because it is a fight you know, right?

Now this next part about the challenge can be interchangeable – used for groups or individuals, In this case, we are going to talk about it as a team effort – both individually and in a group. And I am going to use two different examples – one that in a way was specific to our office and to the overall case management section of the company. But they are examples that are common to most offices/companies.

Documentation and client growth/census or in simpler terms - paperwork and sales...

I put this in our individual section because even though the whole team would have to buy into my plan, each individual would have to do it. I would need to; *"inspire, engage, encourage and empower"* each one individually, for the whole group to be successful.

For us, we couldn't take the time do accomplish one and then work on the other. We had to do them both at the same time. This was not going to be easy – we would have to pull off an amazing feat!

By the time the plan for these challenges was put into place I had been working with them for about four months and had a fairly good handle on what motivated each of them; time with family, recognition, respect and financial rewards, to name a few.

My decision was to begin with the documentation and then quickly and nonchalantly sneak growing the census in the mix. I already knew what the problem with the documentation was – they had told me the first day I was there, inconsistent and wrong information.

We had fixed much of that but what we had to do now was a step beyond that. What *they* had to do now was not just *know* what they were supposed to do but, to *do all of it* - in the proper time frames and with no mistakes. Hah!

This is where working with each one individually was crucial – each one had a different reason why they weren't working to their potential and getting that A+ on their report card.

Let's continue with Diamond as the example. As a case manager Diamond was a great advocate and had passion about her clients and that's exactly what they needed. But, Diamond was very angry.

When she was hired she received almost no training. She was just thrown in the field because a "body" was needed to do the work. She was expected to do the same quality and quantity of work the other case managers did, (the ones who were social workers or nurses) but only get paid about 60% of what they got paid.

Wouldn't you be angry too, getting paid less but expected to put out the exact same amount and at the same level of excellence as everyone else?

Would you be motivated to do a good job?

Would you be motivated to do it correct, on time and with a great attitude?

And would you be motivated not only to do it on your current clients but then be asked to add more (grow census), which means you have to do more?

I think not. Needless to say, there was much encouraging and motivating going on.

Diamond was the toughest one – so I started with her and continued to work with her all the while I was working with the rest, because it was going to take that long for her to catch up to everyone else! We will talk more about Diamond a little later.

And remember, my ultimate goal for each of them was to; *"empower them to success".*

If they were successful as individuals, the group (office) would be successful which then equals that *"I would be successful."*

Hence, successful leadership…

Once they really understand *you* are always *fighting for them – they* will stop *fighting against you.*

Let me say that again. Once they *really understand* that *you – all the time –* are *advocating for them and their needs, hopes and dreams – they will stop ignoring you and sabotaging you.*

So follow through. You expect them to follow through on what you have given them to do, right?

Well, how about you?

You must be willing to follow through also. It's part of that "respect" thing - you must *give it to get it.*

And to repeat myself, "you can't demand respect".

When you demand – respect it not what you get coming back to you. Dutiful compliance laced with discord and resentment is what you get. You must *earn* their respect - you must **plant** respect and loyalty so you will *reap* **their** respect and loyalty, respect equals loyalty.

p.s. Don't forget, all along the way to "be their advocate". Never stop doing that.

Let's review: Love, Faith & Belief and Trust = Engage - Encourage – **Empower**

CHAPTER 2

Working with a Team

The mistake most leaders make is that they think working with a team or a group is different that working with individuals. It's not. The truth is – you don't work with a team or a group, you work with individuals. And, *if you don't work with each one individually, you lose.*

On the other hand – you lead a team, you lead the group. See the difference?

No? Good – there is hope for you!

The realization is that you are working with different individuals with difference life experiences, different job experiences and levels of education, different personal goals, different career goals and very different expectations.

Here's an example. I will use a situation that I am very familiar with and one, I think, you can relate to – mandatory education.

Let's say that I have to get a large group, (approximately 150) to do 14 mandatory educational in-services which are required for anyone working in a skilled nursing facility. And I have many different categories of employees to try to motivate (i.e. nurses, administrative staff, certified nursing assistants, housekeeping, laundry, dietary, maintenance, activities, physical therapy, speech therapy, occupational therapy, nursing supervisors and facility managers).

My goal is to get 100% of these people to be in compliance and do all 14 in-services.

What are my problems? What are my roadblocks?

Some of the material is not directly related to their job, so about 15% view it as unimportant. Another 15% have never had to do this before, (their previous jobs didn't require it). So, this group also views it as not very important. Another 5-10% do not want to do it, because, well - let's call it nonconformity (they also view it as unimportant).

The remaining 60% want to do it or at least are okay with doing it but have to fit it in their already busy, over-worked and over-stressed lives. Oh, and I forgot to mention there's a deadline.

What to do? What would you do and how would you do it?

For me, I realized I had to get all my rowers rowing their oars in the same direction so we could move this boat down the stream, (merrily, merrily, merrily down the stream – life is but a dream…). Hah!

The first thing I did was to engage (ask) several of the employees that I really respected for ideas. Two or three brains are definitely better than one. We came up with an answer, an in-service fair – much like a job fair. In this way we could deal with a large number of people at one time and move them through quickly.

We spent time thinking about the days and times we would have it, the details and the potential pitfalls BEFORE we made the announcement and put out a memo to the whole facility.

This memo was not only posted but went into everyone's paycheck envelope which was a week before the in-service fair was scheduled. Long enough to give them time to coordinate, but not too long so they would forget.

Our premise was - we would set up tri-boards with the mandatory information on them and then have sign up sheets and a quiz for each of the employees to do on all 14 subjects. People could move at their own pace through the boards, ask questions and absorb the information while getting themselves and our facility into compliance. We scheduled a supervisor to be there to answer questions, compiled a list of employees and what in-services they each needed and developed a check-off form for every person which would go in their employee file when all quizzes were completed.

The memo we posted was very important. It had to be informative and it had to include the "why" we needed to get into compliance and, it must be snappy and fun.

The day before we hung several bright signs marking the area they would be taking the quizzes which included written instructions so they would be prepared. The next morning, we set out bowls of candy and handed out funny stickers as a reward for completing the quizzes, similar to what happens when you vote – afterwards a "I voted" sticker is slapped on your chest.

The key word here is "FUN", make it fun.

Making it fun, making it interesting will bring about your success much quicker.

In addition, we elicited the help of our administrator and several other department heads to be some of the first employees in line to participate. Managers *must* be examples and getting the heads of the different departments to make a big "splash" as *they* did the in-services, *was the visible "encouragement" to the rest of the staff.*

Hey, if the leaders aren't willing to do what is needed, why should the employees?

It can't be, "Do as I say, not as I do". It must be, "I am willing to do everything I ask my staff to do". That's what they are expecting you to do anyway. So get in there and get your hands dirty!

We spent time talking and joking with staff, which not only helped to get it done and made it less "humdrum", but was a *great relationship builder and morale booster.*

When the two days were done I looked at what had been accomplished and put out a follow-up memo thanking and praising them for how far we had come. We had gone from 3% compliance to 65% in those two days.

Then I looked at the "who" who still needed to comply. How was I going to get this group in line?

The second phase of my plan was to have a way for the remaining staff "not to have an excuse not to do it". In other words, I had to eliminate their "way out". I had to eliminate the, "I couldn't do the in-services because…factor".

Another important thing, I knew before I started the percentage of staff I hoped to get to participate in the first phase and the *how, when, where and how many* would participate in the second phase. Be prepared! The only question would be, "Would my calculation be right-on, or way-off?"

Since I had my list of staff still needing to complete all the in-services, I again included a memo in the next payroll naming these individuals and I posted a memo letting them know the boards would be available around the clock and set up in a special room with a box to put their completed quizzes in. There would be no supervisor there to answer questions, but if they had any, we were just a phone call away.

Before I go any further, I need to clarify how the tri-boards and the quizzes were constructed. Since we were dealing with all levels of education, backgrounds and job descriptions - I really took my time in putting the boards and the quizzes together.

They had to have the appropriate information on them and presented in such a way that was easy to understand, but not childish. They had to be educational, but interesting enough to keep their attention *and* their respect.

Never underestimate the importance of getting and keeping your staff's respect, without it – you might as well go work somewhere else. You eventually will need to anyway - because you will not succeed!

And, what about those quizzes?

Well, they needed to be short and easy to understand, straight to the point and matching what was on the tri-boards. Again, not as easy as you might think – much time and thought has to go into each project you do, very important!

So, back to getting the remaining 35% on board, or more precisely - on with the tri-boards! With the second memo and a room for the tri-boards to be set up for 24 hour use, in less than a month we were at 98%. Just a few stragglers remaining for the administrator to deal with... success!

This is probably a good time to repeat the importance of on-going coaching and mentoring. If you aren't doing both of those daily, you won't succeed. So, even on your busiest days – you must make time to "experience an *encourage encounter*".

If you don't do it daily and make it important daily, it won't happen and soon you will realize it's been a week, a month or longer – and you haven't done it.

You realize you are out of touch with your staff and out of touch with the one thing, (*the only thing*) that will make you successful – *encouragement!*

Clue #1 – *Beware the person you ignored today – they may be the exact person you need tomorrow.*

Clue #2 – *Know which side the bread is buttered on.*

Clue #3 – *Don't bite the hand that feeds you.*

Clue #4 – *Be kind to everyone as you go up the ladder – you will meet them again. They will be climbing past you on their way up OR they will be kicking <u>you</u> on <u>your</u> way <u>down</u>.* Either way, Clue #5 applies:

Clue #5 – *We reap what we sow.*

Can you handle the truth?

If so, here we go –

Clues 1, 4 and 5 are the same – just presented in a different way. And, you guessed it, 2 and 3 are the same but different, too. Let's discuss…

Everyone is important – from your boss to those hard-working people who sweep the floors and empty your trash. You need them all. So as you are spreading your positive strokes, encouragement and smiling face – don't forget anyone. Don't think that you don't need *everyone*, you will be wrong.

Moving on, change is inevitable.

Change will happen with or without you. If you are prepared and have a plan you will move with the change, if not – "Bye-bye Yellow Brick Road". So as people move up and down the ladder (including you), your trip up and your trip down will be easier, more productive and even award-winning if you have been kind.

Now *kind* is a funny word – not funny ha, ha – but funny - ironic.

We can be kind in the traditional sense – understanding, accommodating and encouraging. An example might be working around someone's schedule due to child care issues. Or, we can still be kind even though we may have to terminate an employee before they make a mistake that can cost money and even lives.

Kind isn't wimpy, kind isn't weak or passive. Being kind in every situation is hard work but can take you from mediocre to extraordinary in your leadership.

And the reaping of what we have sown?

Well, if you give people crap – you will get it back, probably worse than you gave.

The clues about the buttering of the bread while not getting your hand bitten off are about boundaries. About knowing how far you can go with pushing new ideas, advocating, "smoozing" and disciplining. The only way to do this well is to know your boundaries, have a plan and a back-up plan for when your first plan doesn't work.

You know – Plan A and Plan B.

You really can do this. And if you do, you will be able to get anyone to do just about anything for you. And if they really couldn't do it this time – next time they will make sure they do, (my encouragement to you).

Several other areas to pay close attention to: the amount of stress your team has – can they handle anymore? Are you being unrealistic? Are you building your team up or are you tearing it down, *tearing them down?*

Telling them to do something that they know, you know and they know you know is unrealistic – *is stupid.* They won't respect you, they will be angry at you and either ignore you or undermine you. In short, don't do it!

Learn when to back off and back up.

Back off – when you can see in their eyes they are so stressed that they are on their #8 out of their 9 cat lives and are ready to go down for the count.

Back up - re-think the situation and let some time go by. Then reword what you are asking them to do. Most importantly, would you do it? If not, back to the drawing board you go.

Maybe you are being unrealistic.

Maybe you haven't thought it through enough. Maybe there's a better way and you have been so lost in, "being in charge" that you have lost touch with the real "work world" and have been too proud to ask for suggestions, to ask for help.

Stop! Stop, *before* you make an irreversible mistake. And yes, there are some mistakes that are irreversible. Most employees will forgive a few mistakes – unless it pushes their security button. Then you have crossed the line. Don't mess with their money, time with their family or their ego, (too much).

Time management – get your team to tell you. Let them set the number so they own it. And speaking of time management – yours better be great because juggling all this, "ain't easy"!

And goal-setting, everything you do, everything – must have a short and long-term goal to shoot for, a goal to reach so you can celebrate.

And celebrate you must!

Fun, thought-provoking and team-building – all celebrations no matter how big or how small are steps along the way to your success as a leader.

Ask for help. Ask for *their* help.

Nothing makes a person feel included and special more than you asking for their opinion, recognizing their worth and their expertise.

And don't forget to thank them – verbally on the spot of course, but also during a meeting or in a memo for the whole team to witness. This makes the individuals and the team more responsive to you, more willing to participate and follow – you!

You need their ideas and you need their feedback. Otherwise you will be leading a team that does not exist.

Let's rephrase that – you will be leading a team that only exists in your mind and on paper, a fantasy team. And I don't mean Fantasy Football either. It's not the team you need to do the job, *the job your success depends upon.*

So don't lead an imaginary team because soon you will have an imaginary job.

Team building is tricky too. Many of the exercises for it are time consuming and can be b-o-r-i-n-g. Don't do that to them. You will lose them. Be smarter than that, be subtle. Don't let them see that you are trying to get them to work together and be a team. In this way even your most contrary employees can be incorporated into the team.

Several times a week I go around our building and offer a small snack, (an hour before lunch and at mid-afternoon – great "pick-me-up" times). Sometimes I hand out Nutty-Buddy bars or Swiss Cake Rolls - both come two in a package.

When they pick one, (and I carry them around in a very large, pink plastic margarita glass – FUN), I tell them they must share with a buddy.

Nutty-buddy, share with a buddy – get it?

Another good one is to ask one of your team to do you a small favor – like delivering a form to someone or returning a notebook to another part of the building. Better yet, something FUN – like passing around candy or raffle tickets for a door prize you will be handing out at the monthly staff meeting.

Build that team!

One person at a time, one day at a time – each and every day.

Don't wait to "plan" team building. You must make it what you do. What you do everyday and who you are as a leader, who you are as a person. *It must be your character as a leader – a successful leader.*

It's also imperative to set the team boundaries – a code of conduct. People may tell you they don't like rules and boundaries but that is just their mouth doing the talking.

Their heart and soul are saying something else.

You must always be listening for that "something else" hiding beneath their exterior, their mask.

Your team *really does* want to know where you are drawing the line that they can't cross. Even the ones who say they don't' care, they are lying – they do care. In fact, most of the ones that say they don't are the ones that care the most.

Important to remember that – it will help you when you have to respond back to them. Don't get in a spitting match with them. Your job is to outwit them *and help them help themselves.*

Remember Tom Cruise as Jerry McGuire, "Help me, *help you*". If it's good enough for Jerry McGuire – it's good enough for you!

Help them understand they are not only responsible, they are *accountable* for what happens to them if they don't ask for help and do the wrong thing - if they don't follow through, if they don't take the initiative.

Teach them to be able to do their job without you – *that is the ultimate goal.*

For them to get so good at what they do and can anticipate what you want – that you don't even have to show up to work and it get's done perfectly. That should be the goal of every successful leader – you have led them to be *"self-leaders".*

That's the empowerment, that's encouragement without limits – that's biblical.

And lastly, conflict. You will have it, so you better know how you are going to handle it. Everyone needs to know how you are going to handle it. It's best to handle it fast and move on. Waiting – stresses you and leads the team to feel you can be manipulated and weaker than you are. Plus it immobilizes the team, the project and interferes with your success.

Let them know how you will handle it and follow through. Don't complain about it, don't gossip about the gossipers who are complaining about it and don't reward the "conflicters" by gossiping and complaining about it.

Set the example – be the solution, not part of the problem.

Pay attention to the environment you are forcing your team to work in.

Is the environment setting you up for failure? By environment you need to include the equipment and any other resources they will need to do the project successfully.

Again, *ask them* – they know the answer already.

Let them help create the environment they work in.

It's called accountability, which is your job to coach and mentor them into. The blame game is gone, right? That goes for everyone!

Some additional thoughts:

DON'T CRITICIZE – mentor, coach and teach

LISTEN – keep your eyes and ears open

BE WISE – pay attention to your gut feelings

INTEGRITY – wear it for all to see

FAVORTISM – don't do it

TEN – count to it before you speak when you are upset

ANGER – no one's friend

VISUALIZATION – see it before you do it or say it

DISCERNMENT – get some, can't succeed without it

INTIMIDATION – don't do it and don't let others do it

MOTIVES – everyone has them, find them out, what's yours?

CONFIDENTIALITY – don't break it

KNOWLEDGE – your team deserves ALL the information

ADVANCEMENT – belongs to everyone, figure how to do it

THEM – your team is the goal, not money, census, etc…

INSANITY – what you will have if you don't change

HIRING – are you hiring for the short-term or long haul?

CUT BAIT – don't manage the unmanageable

BACK-UP – cross-train, plan for the potential problems

FOOD – never underestimate its' power

PURPOSE – help them find theirs

THANK YOU – say it often

TIME – theirs is as important as yours

NO and YES – both are part of your vocabulary

HELL NO! – if you wouldn't do it, don't ask them to

TIMING – is everything

SMALL – there are no small things, just people (don't' be one)

SMILE – if you are faking this too often, get another job!

THE TRUTH – it is what it is, whether you believe it or not

PRAY – <u>only</u> if you are willing to listen and do what God tells you to

GOD – God manages – you are just the conduit, remember that!

CHAPTER 3

Working with Your Contemporaries

This may be just about the most treacherous group of people you will ever meet - they are all vying for the coveted spot next to the boss. Now, there are two kinds of contemporaries – the ones on their way up and the ones on their way down.

Which do you think is the most dangerous? The people holding on to what they have or the people panting like a rabid dog pulling on the chain tightly wrapped around it's neck trying to "get theirs"?

One is desperate and willing to do anything, the other is ruthlessly driven and relentless.

Both will try manipulation – some will succeed, some won't.

Neither will stay where they were, nor stay where they are now, for long.

Because staying glued to the boss' butt is like straddling a picket fence with prickly cacti on both sides – eventually they're gonna get jabbed and stabbed!

So the one that was relentless is now desperate and hot behind their trail is "another brick in the wall" who is relentlessly manipulating the demise of the desperate one's downward spiral.

How do I know this?

Simple, I pay attention.

Plus I've been the boss and also the one ascending and descending the ladder.

Most people doing this "manipulation dance" are very obvious to others, but totally oblivious to themselves. Which makes them really convincing as they use denial mercilessly. And the really good ones, well they believe it themselves which gives them an extremely high level of believability. And to them – that appearance is everything!

It can be an amazing thing to watch unless you have a conscience or you are the one they are manipulating (and winning), and now it is affecting you.

In my 20+ years in management I've only seen two who I would give the title of "master manipulator" too. Both are women, of course. Men usually use a different tactic, intimidation or con – straight forward in a *"sociopath"* way.

But let's talk about the women.

The first one, let's call her "Ms. Sorority", uses her feminine wiles on the men who are above her, her superiors or bosses. The second, let's call her Ms. Checkmate", plays people like a chess game, moving them around the board, (work place) like so many chess pieces until the Queen is in jeopardy. And, when she finally yells, "checkmate" – it's a surprise, you didn't see it coming.

Now Ms. Sorority is very obvious but it doesn't matter that she is very obvious because she is only very obvious to women, and the boss is not a woman – he is a man. So, he is clueless.

In my situation with Ms. Sorority, I fought her, told the boss about her but with only very limited and temporary success. I had to go through this dance many times. She would get mad and not deal with me (lucky for me), and do her job for a while – then the problems would start again. She would do her "womanly wiles" routine – lying and flirting to cover up, I would fight and tattle and the merry-go-round would continue. All the while, she was telling the boss she could do a better job than me.

This went on until my time was up at that job and God moved me on and out. And yes, you guessed it, they gave her my job.

She got what she wanted and they got a mess. You see, she wasn't qualified for the job, didn't know or understand the job and refused to let me train her for the job before I left, (because she knew it all, of course).

Oh yeah, Ms. Sorority's are also "know-it-all's. Thousands of lost revenue later, they realized the truth. Funny thing about the truth, it will either come out or get covered up – in this case, it was buried.

Ego's – you gotta love 'em.

This was an example of successful leadership – not! Not for anyone.

Ms. Checkmate is more subtle, and more aggravating. She is slippery and just when you think she's been caught, she wiggles her way free. Even when she's wrong – she's right, and you end up scratching your head and wondering what happened.

Sometimes she'll fight openly, only if she's cornered. But her real expertise is behind the scenes. She's often quiet, too quiet – even demure. She hordes information, acts surprised when others are confused, an award-winner at lying and can never be wrong. She's very free to point out others' mistakes, of course, but acts obvious to hers.

She's also a chameleon, switching from an enemy to "being your best friend". She's ambidextrous that way, a conventional "rightie" *and* a "southpaw". The only way to beat her is to be just like her. She's definitely a "keep your enemy closer" type of person. About the only satisfaction you can get, is to snicker behind her back when she messes up and shake your head in frustration when she gets out of it.

Go figure.

This will continue as long as she and you are there – she'll never change, it's in her nature. This is a very important point to remember.

Some people will never change, n-e-v-e-r – ever!

The best you can do is to play the game that is the best for you, for others and for your conscience. The only way she'll get fired is to do it to herself, which happens rarely, or quit – not likely, as she believes she's the "big" fish in a little pond where she has been grazing for a long time. Moving on would be too much hard work of figuring it all out again, she's already got that covered.

My way of dealing with "Ms. Checkmate" is to be nicer, checkmate… And keep my eyes wide open!

Biblically, you have to love these two – *but you do not have to like them.* They both are lost and need prayer, but don't realize it. Often, they will spout about being "spiritual" themselves – leaving a bad taste in the victim's mouth and giving a bad name for those who truly are trying to do the right thing.

The answer? Believe in the "we reap what we sow" principle – it's about the only thing that will get you through it. And if the principle is right, and it is – someday the crop will catch up with the planting!

On the positive side, you will discover some great contemporaries and possibly a friend or two along the way. And if you treat them with respect, consistency and honesty, you can hold your head up high no matter what happens.

Contemporaries should be team players and that is really needed, no matter where you work. Teamwork – and a great team are invaluable. So to be a team player yourself with your contemporaries - give in if you are being stubborn, give up the idea that you always have to be in charge, give up the idea that you are always right – be an encourager and encourage *them.*

Because as we all know, if we have ever lead anyone or anything, *NO ONE encourages the leader.* Satisfaction and the knowledge of what we've done, is our closest friend and the only encouragement we are going to get.

Bottom line – let it go.

Remember, you are not just creating and leading a team – you are part of a team – or you should be. And to be able to be part of the "team", which means working with your contemporaries, you must let their shortcomings and their mistakes roll off your back.

If you can't, or won't - *then go lead somewhere else.*

But when you do, be ready for the same wherever you go. There is no "perfect" workplace and if you find it, you are managing yourself on a deserted island in an "imaginary scenario".

And don't forget the famous words of Michael Corleone, "Keep your friends close, but your enemies closer".

It works here too!

It's biblical – Judas, right?

When Contemporaries Turn Into Your Employees

What happens if you get promoted? That's a good thing, right?

You'd think so, wouldn't you, but it can be a nightmare disguised as a pay raise – if you are not prepared for the fallout.

What's the fallout? Well, let's see…

Depending on what kind of promotion will directly coincide with the number of problems you now have. Remember all those contemporaries that you confided in, vented on about "upper management" and then boasted, *"If I ever became the boss I would…."*

Well, guess what?

You now *are* the boss and all those promises you made – *you have to live up to them.*

All those complaints about management not understanding and knowing what they were asking was impossible to do - now you are management and now if you ask them to do it - *they know that you know* – it can't be done.

And remember whispering about which one of those "bosses" you disliked the most and had no respect for?

Well, they are now your new contemporaries and your *old contemporaries* won't let you forget it – or better yet, they will rat you out to someone. And the person they rat you out to, may even be a bigger rat then the first rat, so look out!

And don't forget – your old bosses may *now* be your *new* contemporaries. Whew! Is this musical chairs? How can we keep this seating chart straight?

So, what do you do? How do you enjoy your new position and be able to walk around with your head held high, get the respect you want from all of them and not always having to look over your shoulder for the knife in your back, or the price on your head?

Simple… Take a page, or two, from the bible.

Take a lesson from David and King Saul.

No matter what David did – someone was mad or jealous of him. Of course, it probably didn't help that he was attractive, had a great personality and bold. *And that of course*, God had chosen him as the next king.

He was a great leader (especially in the beginning before he lost his focus), so we will concentrate on those early years. And besides loving to play music, sing and dance – he also loved the Lord. He believed what was right – *was right*, no matter what. And if he was on the Lord's side and God was *with him* – nothing was impossible – he couldn't fail.

That is where you need to be, where you need to get – to that precise point where nothing is impossible – where all things are possible with God and if it's God's will, you can't fail – you won't fail.

IT IS IMPOSSIBLE TO FAIL.

And since right is right no matter what, then you must do what is right – no matter what people say or think about you. You have to have the *confidence in yourself*, the courage to continue on – no matter what slings and arrows are slung at you. Put that armor on from head to toe everyday and fight your battle.

If people try to sabotage you – don't react with anger or revenge, do the right thing, no matter what. Remember, "We reap what we sow" and eventually you are going to reap a good and positive outcome if you continue do the right thing, plant the right thing.

And your opponent? Well, they will reap what they have sown, too – strife. It's now or later, we don't get to choose which one, but it will come. Reaping always follows sowing, its reality – it's an agricultural thing, and a biblical thing too.

Because if it truly is your purpose to be that "boss", that "upper-level supervisor" then you will come out the other end. You will make it through the rough and tough spots and get to do those things that you said you wanted to do, *"if you ever became the boss"*.

And feed them.

Feed them food, feed them education, feed them respect, love and encouragement *and the opportunities to advance and be empowered to live out their purpose.*

And then no matter what else happens, even if they hate you – *they will love you, too.* Like parents, you do what is best for them because you care, you care about *them.*

It's about *them* – not about *you,* remember?

And if you lead as if it is not about you but about *them* – then they *will* follow – you will be a successful leader and a leader of integrity. And you haven't destroyed anyone. Because as the story of David goes; it wasn't his place to dethrone Saul – that was God's job. David kept doing what was right no matter what and that was his choice.

This is our choice. It has to be our choice if we say we want to lead using biblical principles. No room for hypocrites! So don't be one.

And by the way - who are you leaning on? Who are you asking for advice and who do you trust?

Is it God? Or are you running around asking everyone what you should do and giving away your power, giving away your right – the right to fulfill your purpose.

Hey, don't give away your power – the power that God gave you to do this "thing" – this promotion, this "boss" thing.

This is biblical and I am assuming you want a biblical answer since you are reading a book based on biblical principles and called "The Barnabas Touch", right? If so, then your source is God, it always is.

But the question is; "Do you trust God *enough* to only ask *Him, listen* for the answer and then *do* what *He* says"?

Hmmm… Well, do you?

I hope so because, *He is the answer – He is always the answer and He always has the answer – you just have to ask.*

So, pray for guidance, wisdom and discernment.

Your <u>full</u> faith and trust should be saved for Him, for God - don't waste it on humans, we're flawed.

Remember, with humans, with your employees - you have faith that they will do what you have trained them to do, but you keep your eyes open. That's *you* being a *smart leader.*

But with God, you can put your *whole faith*, your *full faith in Him,* close your eyes, take a deep breath and *know He* has the plan – *your job* is just to *do what He has trained you to do!*

I want to share an example with you about this *"contemporary - to boss thing"* and then I want to explain the "feed them" concept more fully.

So, here goes.

Twenty-nine years ago I became a nurse and started my first job at a 239-bed long-term, skilled facility in Austintown, Ohio. I started out as a part-time LPN (Licensed Practical Nurse), and within four years was the Director of Nursing. Going back to school, graduating Youngstown State University and a stint at St. Elizabeth Hospital helped fill the gap and was the bridge that brought it all together.

During those years, I worked directly as a contemporary with the same people I was now going to have to lead – two different sets of dynamics and two different sets of "respect" buckets.

Even though I had gone through two grueling Directors of Nursing with these nurses, my contemporaries, and even though we had worked shoulder-to-shoulder through short-staffing, emergencies and summers with no air-conditioning, (real blood, sweat and tears) – *I was now their enemy.*

I was their enemy because I was now their boss. I knew too much about them, (how they worked – or didn't), their mistakes and their philosophy of "management" and now, I had control of them. What will they do?

Better yet what would I do?

Well, the one thing I did know is that I didn't want to be like my two predecessors; Ms. Schizophrenia and Ms. Mean-as-hell. And really, that's all I knew. The nurses on-the-other-hand, knew a lot. They knew *my* philosophy, *my* mistakes and how *I* worked.

Now, as usually happens in these transitions, there were several camps of critics; the "she's okay and I will give her the benefit of the doubt", the "well, it's better than Ms. Schizo or Ms. Mean-and-Ugly, and the "I'm scared, so I will try to make *her feel* insecure, unloved and remind her of her flaws – *to protect myself*" critics.

All I could think to do was to ignore them, in a nice way.

I pretended that I didn't know some were trying to suck up to me. I pretended I didn't know some were being "catty" and trying to make me feel unsure of myself - I pretended all of this didn't bother me. I had to pretend because it did matter – I'm human.

After a short while the people who were afraid or just didn't like me got over it or they left. The people who tried to flatter me into promoting them realized I wasn't playing their game and stopped trying and the ones who were on board with me from the beginning or at least giving me a chance, continued to be the strength and the backbone of my ability to lead and get the rest of the followers to follow.

Never let them see you sweat.

Never let them think *they* have *you* over a barrel. That will drive them crazy and it will also make them stop. If they know they can't get to you – the fun is over and they will move on to someone else. Don't give away your power.

Let me say that again, "Don't give away your power".

Smile, sing, whistle or just be very quiet and calm, whatever is your "go to" method. It's like being a method actor, a true character actor. What character are you going to be today? A successful leader can play them all.

Now you may be saying, "This sounds phony, it doesn't sound like Barnabas or engage, encourage and empower to me".

Well, let's dissect it.

If you allow them to upset you – you will react and not act.

Reacting is playing the game, the game of the no-win, no-win situation. Nothing can move forward, *you* can't move forward until the game stops. *You* can't be encouraging or empowering while the manipulating game playing is going on. You have to stop it. You can't forcefully stop it, that's reacting. So you must act in such a way that you cause the "bad behavior" to stop.

You are the catalyst. You are the one who has to do something different. It's all about you at this point.

You have to lead "through" the stuff, the annoying stuff. Once you do, then you can engage, encourage and empower. While you are in the "reacting" mode it's impossible to do this. You may try, you may even think it's working – but you are being fooled. Fooled by yourself because, everyone else knows that it's not working – *you are just in denial.*

Second example, when I worked at Willingway Hospital, the first Alcohol and Drug Rehabilitation Center in Georgia, (and wonderful, too) I started as a staff nurse. After about a year and a half the Director of Nursing resigned and I took her place. One nurse quit and another (who was my best friend there), barely talked to me. Both had been there longer than me and both really had more experience than me "clinically", but that wasn't what they needed.

What did they need?

They needed someone with "leadership" experience, leadership ability – the ability to lead others without the "chaos". Neither of them could do that.

Again, acting as if I was oblivious to what was going on "behaviorally" with these two was the best option. Everyone else was on board and things went fairly smooth. So, I had to put my personal feelings aside. I had to put my "hurt feelings" aside and it *did* hurt. It hurt that the co-worker who I had went on vacation with, went to dinner and the movies with and built a great relationship with – was gone.

But that is the life of a leader.

If you are *meant to be* a leader – you will rise to the top. You will no matter what, because you are programmed to do so. It is who you are. It oozes out of your pores. It comes through when you speak. It comes through when you think – your thoughts and ideas are thoughts and ideas of a leader.

You just have to work on the "being successful" part. Because there's only two choices for a leader – successful or unsuccessful, which one will you choose?

And before I forget – don't *you* forget to be a *Barnabas* to yourself.

Now the "feed them" part.

You must feed them literally and figuratively – both, is essential.

I make soup.

I love to make soup.

It's cathartic – I get rid of everything in my refrigerator. It is creative – I try to come up with a different concoction every time I make it. And, challenging – I try to make it better tasting each time so the staff will want more.

Now take that soup and apply it to work duties, work responsibilities, orienting, training, correcting mistakes, creating opportunities, having to take something away that they like and replace it with something they don't like or just plain having to take something away, period.

This is where it's time you do some of the work because I am not going to take you through each of the above and apply the *"soup principle"* - you are. So, get out a piece of paper and pen and do it.

Really, I am serious.

You won't be able to do any of these things if you don't start to apply it and assimilate it into your life, your leadership life right now!

I'll wait…

Okay, I'm back and I am believing that you've done all your homework. So, let's move on.

I am a firm believer in education – new information and old information with a new twist. The new twist is explaining why they need to do it, what will happen if they don't do it and what great and wonderful things will happen if they do use this wonderful, exciting new information.

A practical example of this is capturing information for maximum reimbursement.

And for me to explain this, we will take a page of the "long-term skilled care handbook". Let's start with a resident (client), and everyday the care they receive will be documented by several employees in different ways, 1) nurses document the medications and treatments they have done, the needs and assessment of the resident, their pain level, behaviors and vital signs, 2) certified nursing assistants document the personal care given and how much help needed to do it, how much the person ate and drank and their elimination – again documenting how much assistance was needed and 3) therapies, restorative nursing, social services and dietary add their required parts, too.

If the nurses and the certified nursing assistants don't document on the resident one day – there's no reimbursement for that day. Or if they document the resident just needed a little assistance rather than the truth – which is they needed total help in all areas – the reimbursement is significantly less.

Let's make this even clearer and put it into dollars and cents. If out of 100 residents 5 were not documented on daily, in one year the facility would lose – approximately $286,000.00. And if 5 residents were documented as needing assistance rather than needing total care the facility would lose in one year - $15,000.00. Adding those two together totals over $301,000.00.

Well guess what? It happens every day in facilities across the country.

And guess what else? There are the employee raises, better insurance benefits, needed equipment and a more pleasing work environment. And the only thing that needs to be done to remedy this problem, is for all the nurses and certified nursing assistants to document and document correctly.

Simple, right? A no-brainer… So, what's the problem?

You can draw a straight line from no or incorrect care to - lost revenue. So why does it happen so often? Why can't you simply get employees to do it correctly every day? Why is this almost an impossible situation to rectify?

In one word - time.

There isn't enough…

Everyone knows what to do, wants and strives to do it but always can't because of time, and no overtime allowed. Because you see, overtime outweighs a little bit of missing or incorrect documentation. Just a little though because once you hit the point where missing or incorrect documentation begins to outweigh the over-time $$$ - BINGO, you get a phone call and you are commanded to develop a training plan and a training schedule to teach staff what they already know but don't have time to do properly.

You are commanded to find time in your already overloaded and impossible work day to invent time to do this, and of course, with a smile on your face - motivated so you can motivate others who are not fooled for a minute by your enthusiasm, (because they know the truth). It really is impossible.

A few mistakes trumps money, until money $$$ trumps everything

Hmmm…

Sounds like I know this a little too well, doesn't it. Sounds like…

Whoops, reality just popped from the backseat into the driver's seat and now is in control and racing down an icy road sliding and swerving – trying to avoid the 18-wheeler in its path and a head-on collision.

Will you see it coming? Did you see it coming?

What do you do?

Serve dinner – first to yourself, then to everyone else.

Serving dinner is the only thing that will possibly (and I did say possibly) work. Let me explain:

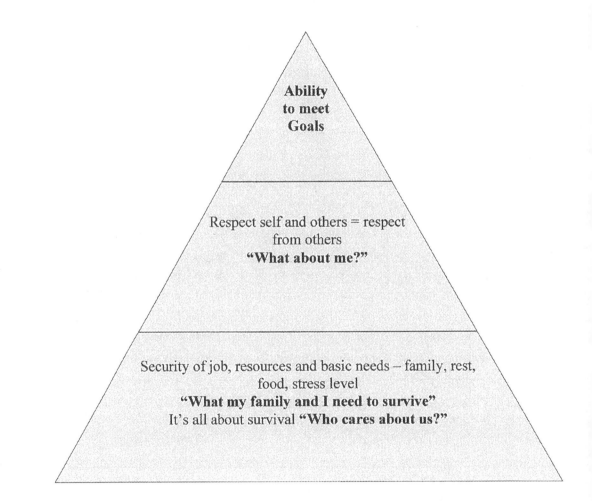

**Ability
to meet
Goals**

Respect self and others = respect
from others
"What about me?"

Security of job, resources and basic needs – family, rest,
food, stress level
"What my family and I need to survive"
It's all about survival **"Who cares about us?"**

Hierarchy of needs as it relates to leading individuals and groups

Taking a cue from Maslow and his hierarchy of needs theory, we need to understand that before we can reach the top, (our goal successfully completed project) we must start working **from the foundation** and **satisfy their needs** – from basic to complex: bills, food, shelter, transportation, spending time with family, sleep and rest.

Otherwise, the **"Who" we lead are unable to do the "What" we need them to do** so that we can turn the **"When, Where and How"** into – **"*Our success".***

Why?

Because people can't think about learning new things and going the extra mile at work if they are worried their electric is going to be shut off, no childcare, their car won't run and they have no way to get to work and the rent is due.

You must realize which of their basic needs are not being met and counteract the negative, what is broken or missing. Find a way to work with them where they are – step into their world.

Bottom line – you will do what you need to do because your bills need paid and your soul, your "feel good" button needs to be pushed. You will do it no matter what – but can you do it "Barnabas style"?

Can you use your purpose to help others realize theirs?

You must, otherwise you are a *"Get-to-the-top-and-stepping-on-whoever-you-can-to get-there"* leader. And that, my friend, really is no leader at all - it's a bully disguised as one.

CHAPTER 4

Working with Your Leader (Boss)

Getting your boss to really trust you is probably one of the toughest things to do. Trust you enough to give up their control and hand it over to you. Trust you enough to empower you to the point where your ideas are their ideas. Trust you enough to give you what you need to get what *you want*.

Trust and enough…

What does trust look like and how much is enough?

Let's start with trust.

Be transparent.

Now that may be uncomfortable for you. It may be scary or make you feel anxious. Do it anyway. Tell them everything you are doing in detail until they don't want to hear anymore. Until they are convinced you actually do know what you are doing and you are as smart as you have been trying to tell them you are.

Ask permission.

Ask permission until they get tired of you asking for permission and tell you not to do it anymore. Until their ego isn't afraid of you and can "trust" (there is that word again), that you are not after their job but you just are trying to do yours successfully and to the highest level.

Don't flatter them.

But do – *acknowledge their successful leadership and ideas,* they are the boss right? They had to do something, (or many things) right to become the boss. Don't forget that. Never forget that.

Never think you are smarter than they are even if in some circumstances you may be. Remember, they are the boss and see the above paragraph.

Don't challenge them in front of even one other person. This is a real deal-breaker. And, even be careful of the "challenging" thing when you are alone with them. Make them draw your opinion out of you – don't just charge in there and give it. Again it implies you know more than they do.

Be a team player.

No matter who they are, what type of boss they are or aren't, they have a lot on their plate. The last thing they need is one more of their leaders who is not willing to play ball – play nice-nice with the rest of the team.

Try not to get mad, let a comment pop out and then leave the room in a huff, (you've guessed it - I've done that one, more than once). But if you find yourself in that precarious situation – go and apologize. Apologize because – YOU WERE WRONG!

It doesn't matter if what was going on was wrong, others were wrong or the wrong was being done to you – don't be wrong too. Don't be part of the problem – it negates your credibility. It is also childish and it takes a long time for others to forget you just made a fool of yourself.

Offer to help them, but do it only if you are sincere.

It is worthless and an empty gesture if you offer "off the cuff" with no meaning. The boss will pick up on that (remember they have had to do these things too, to become the boss), so you really can't fool them, at least not too often.

You may need to be a sounding block for them.

If you are, you must keep their confidentiality. You may be tingling inside to tell someone or shout it from the rooftops – but don't do it! Trust – if you lose theirs – it's a grueling and groveling task to get it back.

They may trust you enough to vent on you. But remember, "It's strictly business, not personal Sonny". Again, a Michael Corleone quote from the most notorious book on business ever, "The Godfather", "Leave the gun, bring the canola's."

And don't try to get away with something behind their back, don't conspire and don't hide. Not only will you lose their trust, you most probably will lose your job – soon!

And from someone who has witnessed this first hand, don't become "personal" or intimate with them. Remember if they are doing it with you they are doing it with others, (sorry to burst your bubble, but you're just not that darn special).

The truth is there is a manipulation going on and you are not the one doing the manipulating.

Enough said.

CHAPTER 5

Working with the Enemy - You

Do you see yourself as your worst enemy, or do you see yourself as your most important ally?

Your answer will define you as a leader – what type of leader you are, how effective you will be or whether people will follow you or not.

Will you be trusted? Can you be trusted?

Will you be in it for the long haul, or are you a one-hit wonder?

The key is mastering *you* – the key is managing and leading – YOU.

You are your biggest challenge. You are the one who will keep you up nights scratching your head and not able to sleep. You are your biggest critic and your biggest enabler. You are the one who will sink your boat faster than anyone else – faster than an exploding torpedo.

You...

And if you can't get *you* out of your head, you will sink – with a *"thud!"*

Let's review...

Why did you say you wanted to be a leader?

What was your reason, what was your answer? The clue to mastering your worst enemy is found in the answer you gave.

If you are doing it for any other reason than you *absolutely know* it is your calling your purpose in life and you are willing to embrace it 100%, then you are sunk. You missed the boat or you are on the boat and it just hit an iceberg.

Either way, you have no boat, there is an ocean of water between you and your destiny and you can't swim.

If you are leading and it's not your purpose – then you never will realize your *true* purpose, the true meaning of your life. You have taken the place of the authentic person who *should* be doing it - and doing it a lot better than you are.

And, there now is a void somewhere in the universe where you should be - fulfilling your purpose in a grand way, but instead someone has filled your slot and are imitating *you* – and *badly*!

So, know *you*. Know yourself.

Once you know leading is where you belong - and this, (whatever this is) is where you should be leading, then never give up and never give in. Never allow discouragement to overtake you. Guard your part of the wall – *Nehemiah.*

And know something else too – when to stop.

When to go home and spend time with your family before they forget what you look like and think their dad is the pizza delivery guy or their mom is, well… their mom doesn't exist. And that's exactly the way they will treat you.

Hey, go listen to "Cats in the Cradle" by Cat Stevens. You'll get the point.

Where are you piling up and storing your treasure?

Don't forget *you.*

You need encouragement, positive feedback, rest and relaxation the same as your staff does. So don't be a martyr - otherwise you will burnout or burn up, useless on both counts.

Forget the guilt.

If you screw up – let them know, "You're human aren't you"?

Thanks Adrian, (Rocky III). They will respect you for it and they will thank you for it. No one likes Mr. or Ms. Perfect – you're a phony if you try to be. You aren't anyway and they know it!

The only leader that anyone will truly follow is a real one, one that is one step ahead of them. Don't be a user and don't allow yourself to be used.

What is my one suggestion to you if I had *only one* to give you?

In all situations ask, "What would Jesus do"?

Not the "perfect" Jesus – the "real" Jesus.

The Jesus who turned over the tables in the temple and the Jesus who expected Peter to walk on the water to Him. *That Jesus* - mixing compassion with correction, boldness with wisdom and never settling for anything less than the truth.

That Jesus…

The Jesus who knew when to rest, when to pray and knew when to flee. The Jesus who rode in town on a donkey, not a stallion fitted in shiny armor and a plumed headdress.

That Jesus… My Jesus… *Your Jesus...*

The Jesus who was not afraid to go in the temple and speak even though he knew the consequences that would follow. The Jesus who quietly said "Come, follow me, I will make you a fisher of men", and he did.

That Jesus…

The Jesus who planned ahead and did not live or minister in "crisis mode", so resist the thought to try to impress the boss and squeak by with "bare bones" staff to save a buck.

You will lose your following, you will lose your respect and you will eventually lose your job because "your" boss will know you don't know what you are doing. Always have Plan B and C, and make sure those plans include hiring, and training in advance and having the foresight to "cross train".

Be the shining star and fight for what you want!

And the Jesus who wept when his good friend died, who confronted hypocrisy when he saw it and who looked for the good in people.

He loved. There was not "like" in Him, only love.

He is the example.

CHAPTER 6

Boundaries in Leadership

"All things work for the good..."

Paraphrase – The Bible

How do you know where to draw the line?

This is probably one of the toughest questions a leader will have to answer.

Where is that boundary marker between being approachable and friendly which equals success and, a too-friendly "open book" now turned into being ignored and completely ineffective?

In my experience, you have to make a few mistakes, learn from them and *never* do them again. It's something that can't really be taught. It can be coached to you, but it is something that the full understanding of it can only come through trial and error.

So let's talk a little about some trials and errors.

First, I want to say that boundaries show up in every chapter of this book – so I will try not to repeat myself by talking about situations we have already discussed. Instead let's focus on success criteria.

Forgive – you must (but you don't have to forget)

Prayer and meditation – daily, otherwise you are driving on an empty tank of gas

Anger management – get some, you'll need it

Stress management – figure out what decreases your stress and do it every day

Communication – make it a life-long love affair, without it all you will get is hate

Spur of the moment "thanks" – pick one person every day and do it, and do it BIG!

Fear Not! They will smell it on you. As Rodney would say, "I get no respect!"

Know when to stop - don't overwhelm, look for blank stares, deer in the headlights

Matrix – design an atmosphere of learning, serving and optimism

Make soup – everyone loves soup

And remember, people may change, motives may change – but *purpose* never changes, yours and theirs.

Purpose has a life, a path – you are just somewhere along the road (or side of the road), of your journey. And so are your employees.

Again, enough said.

Chapter 7

Problems Common to Leadership

Nepotism, don't do it!

Or: "The three reasons why you should never hire your relatives, or your best friend".

One – the other employees won't respect you.

Two – if you don't discipline or fire them when they need it - the other employees won't respect you.

Three – if you do discipline or fire them when they need it you'll live to regret it. The others employees will respect you to your face, (and then laugh behind your back). And you'll have to find a new BFF.

<u>Conclusion</u> – you have a hole in your boat, you are slowly beginning to sink *and* you did it to yourself!

The only exception to this rule is a family business where all the employees are family. Expect the same dynamics at work as you have at home. *And* you can't go to work to escape your family – *they follow you there*!

The employee that everyone feels sorry for, don't do it!

Or: "Why you feel guilty and frustrated at the same time".

And, you can't get your own work done because of the crying, listening to the sob stories and justifications for the lateness and absenteeism. See #1 and #2 from above and then if you do discipline or fire them when they need it you feel bad and the other employees will call you "the big bad wolf" or the "wicked witch of the west".

Conclusion – you have a hole in your boat, you are slowly beginning to sink and you did it to yourself!

The saboteur, don't do it!

Or: "If you have one of these you must make it a priority to seek them out and fire them because they will make success impossible".

If you don't – see #1 and #2 from above. If you do – Congratulations! It probably was an ugly scene with threats of lawsuits, calling state and federal agencies and even bodily harm. Give yourself a high-five and take a day off, you'll need it!

Conclusion – you had a whole in your boat, you patched it. Expect another one to surface. As the leader you are like the little Dutch boy with his finger in the dam – get used to it, it comes with the job.

The "sneaky sniper", don't do it!

Or: "If you have one of these look for the one who always agrees with you, always volunteers and wants to tell you all the gossip".

If you let them into your circle they will secretly become a saboteur.

Fire them!

If you don't, see #1 and #2 from above. If you do – Double Congratulations! Give yourself a high-ten and a week off, you deserve it!

Conclusion – you have a hole in your boat caused by an iceberg, you are on the Titanic and you better find a life preserver because there aren't enough life boats! Well actually there aren't enough life preservers either.

Sneaky sniper had an accomplice and the partner in crime is still there. Look, and then look out!

The "smiling samurai", don't do it!

Or: "This is the employee that smiles to your face then stabs you in the back".

It is about you and "them" and they will take potshots at you until you fire them. They may be the hardest to smoke out but "smoke them out you must"!

If you don't, see #1 and #2 from above. If you do, you will no longer feel bludgeoned and you can quit looking over your shoulder. They will move on, hopefully to your competitor.

Conclusion - smile... Either your boat made it safely to land or it is now lying at the bottom of the ocean and now you can salvage for sunken treasure.

Next is a very important problem common to every business at some time and probably many times - **low or ineffective staffing**.

Don't do it!

Don't let the above holes in your boat remain *employees because "you are afraid you won't have enough staff"* to do the job.

Guess what?

They aren't doing their job now!

Hello...

Someone else is, because they are so busy sobbing, smiling, sneaking, sabotaging, slicing and dicing you up – they don't have time! So take it from me, don't worry about #1, 2, and 3 or the conclusions.

Discipline and fire according to your policy, remember to document it and please – next time do a better job of hiring. Learn how to hire!

And if someone else is doing the hiring – maybe they're the one that needs the firing squad! Maybe they're the one who put the hole in your boat! Ya think?

Now let's talk about ***remembering.***

Have you remembered that "your motivation" is _not_ the same as theirs and if you push them too hard to try to get them to change – you will be leading yourself – they will have gone home, *which was their motivation all along.*

You can only push people so far.

You can only work them so hard.

You can only ask them to give up so much.

And you can only ask them to follow you if you are willing to be a leader who is an example – live it as they are asked to do. Not sit in an ivory tower (your office), and pretend you don't know they are struggling - pretend you don't see the problems and pretend you have asked them to do the impossible.

Workplace romance – "Don't do it!"

On any level it doesn't work – or at least it doesn't work for long.

If you date someone higher on the food chain than you (God forbid it's the boss), it will end at some point unless you get married to them and leave the workplace.

So someone had to end it – the "ender", which leaves the "endee". Someone gets the short end of the stick leaving a very uncomfortable work situation.

If you date someone on a lower rung of the ladder, again it will eventually end, (see above illustration).

And if you date someone horizontal, you both are competing for the same things at work – recognition, power, higher wages and respect. "Something's gotta give!" Or someone, and again it will eventually end – blah, blah, blah…

And lastly be wary of hiring "**couples**". Remember they do everything together – get sick, vacation and attend to sick relative or funerals. *Try* not to do it.

Next…

Okay, this is the perfect place for me to mention the most common problem we all face – **forgetting**.

Forgetting you need to say "thank you" to them. Forgetting these people are people and not "robots". Forgetting they have to eat, sleep and that they have a family and forgetting the most crucial thing; "forgetting to *reward more for the good than you are punishing the bad".*

Everyone does it – but the most successful leaders have learned the secret of taking time every day to focus on ways to reward, *because* - this will leave less time for your brain to focus on how you are going to punish someone's bad behavior.

Now when I say "bad behavior", *for me*, this encompasses several layers of negative actions. It ranges anywhere from; outright mistakes, unthinking goof-ups, gossip, rumors, bullying and strife. It means all things that are getting in my way of succeeding in what I am trying to do and am trying to get them to do.

It is what is standing between me and success. It is what is standing between me and my goal. It is what is keeping me up at night and putting gray hairs and wrinkles in places I don't want them!

Bottom line – if people feel appreciated they will do more than what is expected. They will want to feel appreciated again and again. And, they will surprise you.

They will get so used to you coming around and being positive, smiling and encouraging them – that on a day you aren't smiling or encouraging they will think something is wrong. They may even say to you, "Are you okay?" "Smile…" "What's wrong, you look mad".

That's when you know you were doing something right and now you have forgotten to do it and are *now* – doing something wrong.

So "thank them".

Thank them for pointing it out to you. Thank them for worrying about you, thank them for paying attention – thank them for whatever you want to – just *"thank them"*.

Wednesday I had to fire someone.

She needed it, she had become totally undependable. Do you know what she did? She "thanked me". She thanked me for giving her a chance. She thanked me for giving her the opportunity to learn. She thanked me for caring about her and she thanked me for trying to point out her weak areas and then, giving her ideas and feedback on how to change.

Sometimes they will encourage you and it may be in the most unlikely situations.

Savor it! It is rare, and you may have to live off it for a quite long time before you hear it again.

It's what I call a "tracker".

Like a Geiger counter but measuring *your* level of effectiveness, *your* level of progress and success. It is something that will keep your internal compass pointing "North" – to home, *your goal.*

And what is the goal again?

It's juggling. Yes, juggling.

Juggling the "do's" and "don'ts" to the point where you have forgotten to lead - because it is *who you are* and it naturally just oozes out of you.

You have successfully led your staff to the point where they know what you want so well that they have forgotten they are following you, and –"doing what is right is *who they are"*.

Perfect.

Chapter 8

"Call-ins for Dummies..."

I love this title. It is so self-explanatory.

If you are dumb enough to use any of these call-in excuses than you will not be working for me, with me or anywhere near me.

Dummy call-in excuse #1 – It's Saturday and you are scheduled to work. You have your child call or text me and tell me that you can't come to work because you are in the hospital having tests done on your legs and liver.

Of course, everyone knows Saturday is "leg and liver" day at the hospital. If you can't think of a better excuse than that – then you have watched "Dumb and Dumber" one too many times.

Dummy call-in excuse #2 – You have your child call or text me and tell me you are in the hospital because you broke your foot. Then, the next day you come in to work skipping down the hall like Dorothy in "The Wizard of Oz". And when I ask you about your foot you say, "Oh, the x-rays haven't come back yet" and start limping, (on the wrong foot).

If you can't think of a better excuse than that – you must have been dropped on your head as a child, repeatedly.

Dummy call-in excuse #3 – You have been talking to everyone about needing to have the day off because of something special you want to do. You have asked me to find someone to work for you – I have said "no" – it's your responsibility. The day arrives and you call in sick.

Really?

If you can't think of a better excuse than that – you must think I am really stupid!

Dummy call-in excuse #4 - You call in sick the entire week-end you are scheduled to work AND then you post on your Facebook page what a wonderful time you and your boyfriend had horseback riding over the week-end. What do you think "social media" means?

Like, everyone can see it – hello…your co-workers and your boss!

If you can't think of a better excuse than that – *I can't believe I was stupid enough to hire someone that stupid!*

I could go on and on, but I think you get the point.

CHAPTER 9

Are you an Olympian?

"Command - Don't Demand"

Are you brave enough? Brave enough to use love to encourage and empower others to the top?

I hope so, because that is what it will take.

It will take all your patience, tenaciousness, wisdom, understanding, strength and endurance. You will need to train yourself like a boxer, condition yourself like a long-distance runner and prepare your heart and mind for a triathlon.

Any very importantly, you will need God – you will need prayer.

Because, the same as Mother Teresa, you must see them "through the eyes of "Jesus". You must see the good in them so you will be able to help them overcome the "bad" in themselves.

If you don't believe in spiritual warfare, demons and anointing in oil – please skip this next part:

A number of years ago I worked for a Hospice and I found it to be very difficult for staff to give compassionate care while preparing their client and themselves for the death that will follow, then having to move on to the next lovely soul with no time to grieve.

> *As a result, it often felt like there were little nasty demons running around our office terrorizing our staff with strife. Honestly sometimes we were at each others' throats – like lions on antelopes. When it would get so bad that we really needed a miracle our Chaplain, Social Worker and myself would come in very early one morning and anoint the entire office with oil, and prayer. For us and our office it worked, doing this act of faith made a difference.*

Okay, now you can look again.

Command... Don't Demand!

"M-e-e-e-ster, please explain". I will, Topogeejo. Thank you Ed Sullivan.

Here's me, re-enforcing to you, on this critical principle; let's revisit "respect".

What is the difference between the way people reacted when King Henry VIII walked into the room and when Mother Teresa (or Jesus), walked into the room?

When Henry walked into the room they didn't know whether he was going to exploit them, slap them on the back, put a knife in their back or cut off their head - so they acted with fear and trembling (disguised as respect), because they were terrified.

With Mother Teresa (or Jesus), they knew they were going to be loved and get the help they needed no matter what - *so they gave their respect because they were given respect **first**.*

True successful leaders command respect, they don't demand respect.

If you demand respect you are scared and your employees sense that – like dogs sense fear in humans. They know you have resorted to your last tactic – demanding, because you are afraid of them, afraid to fail and afraid to be wrong.

You have lost.

You have given away your power and are now powerless to do anything but scare them into "obeying" you, submitting to you.

And what do we know about human nature?

Human don't like to be *made* to obey – they don't want to be *made* to submit – they will fight. They will fight you, the team, the project and the company.

Lose, lose, lose, lose – you lost. Maybe even your job, or at least your job as their leader. See the difference? No, be the difference…

It will take belief, faith, trust and a lot of love to engage, encourage and empower your staff so you will be successful. It will also take faith, belief, trust and loving *yourself* so you will be successful.

And without a doubt, it will take belief, faith, trust and love of God for *anyone to be successful.*

Enough said.

So, I'm, asking you again, *"Are you an Olympian?"*

CHAPTER 10

Troubleshooting - Interviews

A smart leader understands interviewing.

A *successful leader* is one who is smart because they understand interviewing *and* hire strictly from the interview – unless of course, they are desperate and just need a body.

Me?

I've been on both ends of that stick!

<u>Trick #1</u> – if the person walking in to fill out an application comes dressed in shorts so short and tight that you can't see where their legs end and their waist begins – don't interview them. If they come in flip-flops – don't hire them. If their hair is greasy and dirty, stringy and uncombed – do not interview them.

You think I am being judgmental? Am I too harsh?

Watch the movie," The Pursuit of Happyness" starring Will Smith. *That* is a person who was willing to go to any lengths to reach his goal.

So, the person who is putting in that application and supposedly wanting you to hire them – do they really want the job? That job – the job you have advertised for, the job that is critical to have the right person in, the job that *your* job hinges on. Flip flops, really?

Think!

Pay attention!

If part of your job is hiring – who hired you?

Did they make a mistake? Or did they hire wisely?

Those we hire are a reflection of us. In other words, we reap what we sow.

Hire a loser – you lose. Hire a winner – you win. Simple as that!

But…But…But…

You can make as many excuses as you want and justify anything – but, the bottom line is - who we hire is an indication of what we think about ourselves, the company and the people the company serves.

Sometimes the truth hurts.

Make "truth" your standard. Do not be afraid to be honest with yourself, and to be honest with them. It is the kindest thing you can do.

Trick #2 - if they get past Trick #1, did they fill out the back of the application or did they say, "Oh I didn't know there was a back to it".

Hey, every front has a back, right? Every front of an application has a back to the application, right?

Hello? Anyone home…

Trick #3 – Did they come prepared to be interviewed?

Did they bring their driver's license?

If they drove their car to your place of business but when you ask them for their license so you can make a copy of it they say, "Oh, I must of left it at home".

Don't hire them!

They just drove to your place of business without a license which means they don't follow the rules, are forgetful, don't care - or they lost their license due to speeding or driving under the influence.

In any of these cases, they are not hiring material. They are someone else's problem not yours – so don't adopt someone else's problem child.

Trick #4 – If you called them to set up a time for an interview – were they on time?

If they were late it is not an automatic "no hire". There could be legitimate reasons why were late. But if they were more than 10 minutes late, did they call to let you know they were running late?

Ah-hah!

If so, they are considerate and respectful of you and your time. If not, this is a pattern, they will be late for work, trust me!

<u>Trick #5</u> – Talk to whoever handed them the application to fill out.

This person will have a wealth of information for you. They have been talking to and observing your potential new hire while they have been filling out the application. Most people don't think about what they are saying and how they are saying it to this person. They are just the receptionist, secretary or administrative assistant, right?

Wrong!

They are your ace-in-the-hole, your secret weapon – so use them.

<u>Trick #6</u> – What did they put on that application? And what *didn't* they put on it?

Can you read it and does it make sense. Do they have the phone numbers and the names of their supervisors to their last several jobs? They knew they were coming to fill out an application – what the heck did they think they were going to put on it – a letter to Santa Claus?

Are there gaps? If so, it's probably intentional.

Did they bring a resume, (give them an extra point). Did they bring reference letters, copy of their professional license or credentials?

Did they bring a pen?

Nothing drives me crazy more than a person who does not bring a pen to fill out the application, to the interview or to the first day of orientation. Didn't they think they were going to have to write or sign something? Are they forgetful, clueless or just plain stupid?

Or do they think we are supposed to supply everything they need – think about that one. Sounds to me like you will be following them around picking up their slack every day - hey, and you did it – you hired them!

<u>Trick #7</u> – Did they bring a whole handful of unruly kids with everything but the kitchen sink trailing behind them?

Again, there can be a good explanation of why they had to bring their children, but – they should have told you while they were making the appointment. Or when they knew they had no choice but to bring them, they should have called and asked you if it was okay to bring them.

Again, courtesy and respect, If they don't have it for you, they won't have it for their job or the people the job serves.

<u>Trick #8</u> – Okay, if they have made it this far they are now sitting down in front of you doing an interview. Are they too talkative? Do they look you in the eye or everywhere but? Are they confident, or maybe too confident?

Are you a good lie detector?

You better be – because this is where you have to get them comfortable enough to forget they are in an interview so the truth will come out and not just what they have rehearsed over and over to say.

You should have at least a two-page written interview with a variety of questions. Some yes and no questions, some one or two words answer questions and two scenarios which they will have to remember an example from their past experience. Also one surprise question – like, "What do you want from *your* supervisor?"

These different types of questions should be in a random order which helps keep the interviewee off guard.

<u>Trick #9</u> – Are they willing to do a drug screen. If the answer is no, thank them and show them the door. If they say, "Oh, I just went before I came or when I got here" Hmmm…

They knew they had the interview, they knew part of the interview was probably going to be a drug screen (especially if it is healthcare related), so what about them <u>not being ready</u> are you going to accept?

Your choice, what do you do?

Trick #10 – Don't hire someone for a director position who is fresh out of school, no experience, who doesn't know there is a back to the application and didn't bring a pen. Unless you are willing to take a chance, because sometimes you have a "hunch" that really pays off.

Okay, so now you have gotten through the first interview and you have to decide – are they worth going any further because you now will have to do a back-ground check, *which costs money.* You will need to take your time, (*which is money*) and call their references (*again time and money*). Sidebar – only call business references (not personal ones), unless you know one of the personal references yourself.

And remember, this process takes time away from hunting for the right person since you probably had to think twice about the one you just interviewed.

But let's pretend you are willing to take a chance and go further with this one. Let's say the background check comes back okay, (and since they were a professional with a license) that comes back okay, too. Which now leaves you at a crossroads – hire, not hire or do a second interview.

If it is a serious position, one that is high-paying, supervisory or someone you will work with directly – definitely, *definitely* (thank you *"Rainman"),* do a second interview.

The second interview should be with someone else, this is crucial.

They have already won you over. So get someone "more difficult than you" to do the second interview. Either someone who will make them nervous or someone who they feel so relaxed with that the "secret" comes out.

Everyone has a secret – did you know that?

You have a secret.

Think about it. There is something that you wouldn't say to an interviewer unless is accidentally popped out, right?

That's why the second interview. Plus it is taking up someone else's time not yours. But most importantly, if they fail the second interview – you have just saved yourself weeks, months even years of agony, headaches and money.

Who-rah!

And, if they do make it past the second interview then you have a very good chance of having a successful hire. One that will hopefully stay past their training and work with the company for a long time – not just take that great training you gave them and parlay it into a better paying job somewhere else.

Hey, and if they don't work out or do the above, (using you) then you have someone else to blame – that *"dang second interviewer!"*

So let's go back and take a look at those flip flops and short-shorts.

Maybe it's a hot day, maybe they are young and this is their first job. And just maybe no one ever told them how to dress when they go to put in an application.

I don't know – you can't always judge a book by it's cover.

It's the same way with people.

They will surprise you, people I mean not covers. I've hired the ultimate "professional" and it hasn't worked out. And I've hired people who looked like they just rolled out of bed or came from the beach and it has worked out fine.

Now I ask you, did you pick out "engage, encourage and empower" in this interviewing process?

This will be the element that separates the good from the *great* leaders. This is what creates *"inspired success"* in leadership.

Let's go back and take a look…

Engage – is this someone you can work with, someone who will allow them self to be led - by you? You must be able to get a sense of this during the interview.

Encourage – is this someone you can love, not necessarily like – but love? Love them into the employee you need them to be? Someone who will allow you to and allow them self to be molded into a team player?

Empower – is this someone you want to take all the time and energy it's going to take to; inspire them into changing, inspire them to inspiring others and inspire them into a leader themselves?

Surprise!

It all hinges on you – not them.

Never saw that one coming did you…

I am not surprised. It took me a long time to understand this to. There is a knowing feeling that you must get during the interview process before you hire them. If you don't feel it – don't hire them.

It feels a little different for each individual. For me, it's a combination of being comfortable and knowing they are responding to me; a marriage of sorts between their ability to listen and follow instructions without an attitude - and without a "total cluelessness".

And lastly, if I feel that all they are doing is interviewing *me* – I know they want what "they want" too much, they believe they are right, and will be too difficult to lead.

But that's me.

You, on the other hand, may feel it differently. But you will feel *something*.

Pay attention to that "something" you feel. Don't ignore the "something" because unless you have known this person for a long time – that "something" is all you have to go on.

Some call it a "gut" feeling.

Well, you may or may not feel it in your "gut", but you better feel it somewhere and to be wise enough to act on it - or you are in for a world of hurt and agony.

And, more interviewing…

Again, realize and utilize *"the three secrets to success". It's your road to successful leadership… and a little peace of mind.*

The End of the Beginning...

I was surfing my 22 new notifications on Facebook, when I came across this statement:

"Before you say something to someone, think how you would feel if it was said to you."

And I realized that is what this chapter is about.

At the long-term care facility where I work as Staff Development Coordinator, we tell our nursing staff to, "Treat the residents as if they were members of your family or yourself – treat them they way *you* want to be treated, the way you would want *your family* to be treated".

It is the same with leadership – *successful leadership.*

You can't just put yourself in their shoes – you must train yourself to - *live in their shoes while you are walking around in your role as leader* or supervisor or whatever title they have given you today.

Let's call it Bi-Polar Leadership – B.P.L.

Really it's more like Multiple Person Leadership – M.P.L.

We have two sides of our brain – the right and the left. So we can make this simple. Just pretend *you* reside in one hemisphere and your workers and co-workers reside in *the other*, simultaneously.

For BPL/MPL to work, you must take it very seriously and work hard at it because that is what we are asking our staff, our employees to do. To put themselves in the place of the person they are caring for, servicing – doing their job for.

So as we have already learned, "If you can't do the job – you can't ask them to do it".

And if you need something biblical to base this concept on – think JESUS.

Jesus was the founder of BPL/MPL. Jesus never talked to people - his disciples, his followers or sinners on the street without thinking; who they were, how they needed to be approached and how they would react.

Our example is always Jesus, and our guide book is the bible. Every page of that book is filled with good and bad leadership examples. Every page is filled with instructions and illustrations and for lack of a better word, "parables".

This isn't something I've conjured up in my head. It's in there.

What kind of leader do you want to be? You'll find it in there.

What kind of contemperary do you want to be? You'll find it in there.

And what type of employee do you want to be? You'll find it in there.

You can either be a follower of the leadership of Jesus or not, *your choice*.

For me, I have realized that my purpose is to *work on me* so that it is *Jesus* that people see. It is Jesus that comes out of me and touches others. *It is Jesus.*

One of my favorite role models is Mother Teresa. Take time to read a book about her, don't just "google" her and read what's on Wikipedia. Really read about her – her life, her heart, her purpose.

She ministered to the poor of the poor, the down-trodden and dying in one of the worst places on earth. There was no reward except – *love*. The more love she gave away, the more she got in return.

There are many inspiring stories about her and beautifully courageous quotes, but the one that comes to my mind when I think about her is this one:

A reporter once asked her how she could do what she did day after day. How could she not get discouraged or too tired to go on? How could she expose herself to the horrors and the disease? Her answer was simple. She said, "When I look at their face, when I look in their eyes – I see Jesus".

Nothing fancy, nothing mystical or nothing academic with a mathematical theory – just love...

Isn't this the way we all want to be seen?

Isn't this the way we want others to look at us – looking for the good, not always looking for the bad? And finding the part of us that wants to do our best - that wants to be a better person, a better human being?

So, for the better human being inside, *"May you have the wisdom to find your purpose, and the courage to make a difference"*.

If you're still breathing, you still have a purpose – *there is* a reason you are here on earth.

What are you waiting for, someone to do it for you?

Sorry, it doesn't work that way.

Next...

What Next?

"Build an ark, the sky's getting dark"

Has the leader you were meant to be risen to the top, or have you realized you need to go back to the drawing board and sketch out a new plan?

Which ever one you have chosen – it's time to do something about it.

It's always about action.

It's always about you. Until you make a move, nothing else will. Until you make a change – everything will stay the same. You are the key – you are the catalyst.

You...

You can have a career of successful leadership, or not.

You can have a career of successful following, or not.

You can have whatever you want, or not. The choice is up to you.

No one is accountable for you except you. Your successes, your failures, your life - *is your life.*

Oh, by the way, did you think I forgot to finish up the story about Diamond and the rest of the crew – the person who really was the problem, the saboteur?

Well, it was the one most unlikely to succeed, the one always "concerned" about everyone and the one always tattling on everyone. She finally showed her face and her "a_ _", and we fired her.

This also helped the rest of the company see the office wasn't as "dumb" as everyone thought. Sometimes you just have to wait for them to "show their hand" – they always do, the losing one.

"You gotta know when to hold 'em, know when to fold 'em, know when to walk away, know when to run", thank you Kenny Rogers and "The Gambler".

I struggled with this next tidbit, but here it is.

If you are working in ministry or contemplating working in ministry, don't be blind-sided; people are still people and all the above applies to ministry, too.

Just because it is ministry does not make people holy or more honest or more trustworthy – it just makes them working in the ministry. So keep both of your antennas up, "wisdom" and "discernment", all the time.

And if you are wondering if this book applies to working and being a leader in the ministry, the answer is yes – it applies exactly in the same way. There is no difference between working in the "world" and working in the "ministry" – the difference is *you*.

You are the only difference. You are always the only difference, no matter where you work.

Life is serious – but don't take it too seriously.

And remember, whatever you look for – you will find.

Don't settle.

Don't settle for ordinary, capture *"extraordinary"*!

Epilogue

"Reach for the stars – the worst you can get is a "twinkle".

- Susan Farah

My hope is writing this book is that I have helped you bridge the gap between leadership and successful leadership – the gap between you and your employees.

To recognize that being a leader is to be a follower of a leadership style. It can be a good one or a bad one, it's up to you.

Barnabas and Jesus are not too shabby of individuals to study, right?

But the bottom line is - there is already a leader in you trying to get out.

Are you going to continue to keep them prisoner or are you in the parole mode today?

Are you giving yourself permission to throw open the cell door, say good-bye to the bars forever and make a bolt to freedom?

Whatever you choose you have to work at it. So why not work at something that will be successful, fulfill your purpose *and* make you feel good all at the same time?

$6.00 worth of cupcakes, that's all it takes.

That's the easy part.

The hard part is to do it. To get off your chair, go to the store and then go to your workplace, (on your day off) and pass out the cupcakes.

And why are we getting up, buying and distributing?

Because you just got a phone call letting you know that you have an *incredible team,* a TEAM that pulls together and makes it happen no matter what – no matter who shows up for work or not, no matter how hard the task – **no matter what!**

Aren't they worth it?

Aren't they worth the time, the effort?

Aren't they worth $6.00?

The Barnabas Touch...

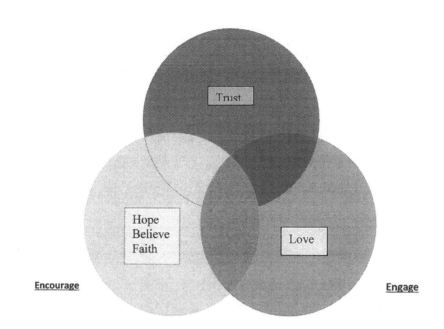

Empower

Trust

Hope
Believe
Faith

Love

Encourage

Engage

E₃ - **Engage** + **Encourage** = **Empower**

Love   Hope Believe Faith   Trust

The **Olympic Rings** of Successful Leadership

Appendix

Successful Leadership Outline and Worksheet

Secret #1 -

Secret #2 -

Secret #3 -

Working with Individuals:

Working with a Team:

Working with Your Contemporaries:

Soup recipes:

Working with Your Leader (Boss):

Working with "The Enemy", You:

Boundaries in Leadership:

Problems Common to Leadership:

Call-ins for Dummies:

Are you an Olympian:

Troubleshooting – Interviews:

Goals (3 short-term, 1 long-term):

#1

#2

#3

#4

Progress on each goal:

#1

#2

#3

#4

Improvements on each goal:

#1

#2

#3

#4

Successes:

Un-successes:

Evaluation:

Re-evaluation:

Ultimate conclusions:

The End of the Beginning – What Next?

Your Epilogue:

Your "Appendix" (tools **you** have **invented** to **accomplish** your **goals)**

Sample Template - Care Plan a Problem "Opportunity"

Plan of care _____

Date	Opportunity	Goal	Date	Interventions	Progress

Will you get a chance to share your faith?

Don't you know?

You do it everyday in every way.

Living out biblical principles is your job, let God do the rest.

Remember, we are his secretary – he is the author.

We just put hands and feet to what he does – what he needs done.

We are not the originator, we are the messenger.

Just be available!

Live your life in such a way that you leave no doubt as to your faith, what you believe.

If you have to talk about it all the time you are not living it. If you are living it – you don't have to talk about it – everyone will see.

www.27EWORDSTHATWILLCHANGEYOURLIFE